LANGUAGE AND LITERACY SERIES

Dorothy S. Strickland, FOUNDING EDITOR
Celia Genishi and Donna E. Alvermann, SERIES EDITORS
ADVISORY BOARD: Richard Allington, Kathryn Au, Bernice Cullinan, Colette Daiute,
Anne Haas Dyson, Carole Edelsky, Mary Juzwik, Susan Lytle, Django Paris, Timothy Shanahan

D0940780

Language and Literacy Series, *continued*

"We've Been Doing It Your Way Long Enough"

CHOOSING THE CULTURALLY RELEVANT CLASSROOM

Janice Baines   Carmen Tisdale   Susi Long

TEACHERS COLLEGE PRESS

TEACHERS COLLEGE | COLUMBIA UNIVERSITY

Published by Teachers College Press, 1234 Amsterdam Avenue, New York, NY 10027

Copyright © 2018 by Teachers College, Columbia University

All cover photos by Susi Long. Cover design by Patricia Palao.

Library of Congress Cataloging-in-Publication Data

Names: Baines, Janice, author. | Tisdale, Carmen, author. | Long, Susi, 1952–, author.
Title: We've been doing it your way long enough : choosing the culturally relevant classroom / Janice Baines, Carmen Tisdale, Susi Long.
Description: New York : Teachers College Press, [2018] | Series: Language and literacy series | Includes bibliographical references and index. |
Identifiers: LCCN 2018014798 (print) | LCCN 2018028089 (ebook) | ISBN 9780807775714 (ebook) | ISBN 9780807757178 (pbk.) | ISBN 9780807757185 (case)
Subjects: LCSH: Culturally relevant pedagogy—United States. | Language arts (Elementary)—United States. | Education, Elementary—Curricula—United States.
Classification: LCC LC1099.3 (ebook) | LCC LC1099.3 .B34 2018 (print) | DDC 372.60973—dc23
LC record available at https://lccn.loc.gov/2018014798

ISBN 978-0-8077-5717-8 (paper)
ISBN 978-0-8077-5718-5 (hardcover)
ISBN 978-0-8077-7571-4 (ebook)

Printed on acid-free paper
Manufactured in the United States of America

25   24   23   22   21   20   19   18   8   7   6   5   4   3   2   1

We dedicate this book to Sonia Baines,
whose love represents the families and communities
whose wisdom, caring, support, and activism
inspire and inform our teaching every day.

To my mother,
you were the first person
to give me what I needed
in order to teach.
I'm re-gifting.

—Janice Baines

Contents

Acknowledgments

First, we express deepest gratitude to the children, families, and community members from whom we learn and who support our efforts to share their words and experiences. We also owe much gratitude to our editor at Teachers College Press, Emily Spangler, whose suggestions strengthened this text and whose patience kept the project alive. Extra thanks go to Gloria Boutte, Nathaniel Bryan, Michael Dominguez, Erin Miller, Kindel Nash, Dinah Volk, and Kamania Wynter-Hoyte, who read drafts of this book or chapters in it and offered wisdom that truly transformed what we are able to say. Below, we each offer acknowledgments to those who make professional and personal differences in our lives every day.

Janice

First, thanks to God for ordering my steps, providing the support, and giving me the strength to complete this task. Thanks to my family and friends for having love, patience, and time. Who knew that our experiences would shape me into the teacher I am? It was all necessary and I am forever grateful. Thanks to my Benedict College Family for coordinating such a valuable teacher education program. The guidance and love they provided will never go unnoticed. Thanks to my Carver Lyon Family for welcoming me into teaching and the first opportunity to be "Ms. Baines." Thanks to my professors at the University of Wisconsin for organizing the Curriculum and Instruction program and embracing my experiences.

Thank you to all other mentors, institutions, and organizations for inspiring me and helping with the shifts made in my thinking. Thanks to my students for entrusting your minds and hearts to me, teaching me, and changing my role so many times. Lastly, thank you, Carmen and Susi, for being you. Words cannot express the love and support you've given me. This has been a long journey, but I learned that the true gift of writing is the process.

Carmen

For me, teaching has always been about building lasting relationships. I am forever grateful to my babies and their parents for entrusting their education to me and allowing me to become "their mama at school." Long after they left my class, they welcomed me into their lives with open arms to do this work. My students helped me grow, change, and realize that love is the driving force of all that matters.

I also thank my parents, Charlie and Jannie Ervin, for always being supportive of any projects I have taken on. Making them proud has always been a goal, because they have given so much of themselves. Giving me everything from words of wisdom to hugs, they are always there to make me feel safe in this world. I love them with *all* my heart.

I am thankful for my dear friend, Nicole Priestly, who provided a sounding board through this whole process. As an educator herself, she allowed me to depend on her to help me think through ideas and make sense when the work did not make sense. She was the voice of reason many times when I contemplated the stories I had to tell.

I am eternally grateful to have a seat at the table to watch the brilliance of my colleagues, Janice Baines and Susi Long. Their humble spirits make me a better person, and I'm in awe of their deep knowledge of children and how they learn every time I'm in their presence. They are my *best* teachers. However, it goes beyond a working relationship. These ladies have become my family. We formed a sisterhood that allowed us to face challenges and have hard conversations.

In the end, I am thankful for my family—my husband, Kenneth, and our daughter, Ariyana. They accepted the fact that the time I spent away from home took away from what I value most—family. I love you both endlessly.

Susi

My deepest thanks go to Janice and Carmen, whose light and love will always remain in the hearts of their children and families. As dear friends and colleagues, they invited me into their classrooms and sat around my dining room table as we explored teaching, learning, and writing together. Our journey continues as they teach, through their example, the definition of unconditional love and patience.

Particular thanks go to colleague-activists who have inspired through the years because of their courage, brilliance, and sense of purpose: Dale Allender, Clavis Anderson, Eliza Braden, Nathaniel Bryan, Ronda Bullock, Roberta Gardner, Marcelle Haddix, Detra Price-Dennis, Tambra Jackson, Shashray McCormack, Gholdy Muhammad, Meir Muller, Yolanda Sealey-Ruiz, Dinah Volk, Rachelle Washington, and Kamania Wynter-Hoyte.

These scholars stand hand in hand with doctoral graduates who are now professors in their own right and whose work teaches me so much: Michelle Grace-Williams, who directed me to decolonizing methodologies; Dywanna Smith, who teaches me never to stand for less than courageous work; Elizabeth Holmes, who taught me about heritage and grace; Kindel Nash, who lovingly nudged me to recognize that I was barely skirting issues of race and encouraged me to learn from Michelle Bryan's life-changing course in critical race theory; and Erin Miller, who is always the best sounding board and led me to seek understandings about Whiteness and racism.

Special thanks to Gloria Boutte, one of my first teachers in this process, whose courage has had a deep impact over many years. Enduring gratitude to Valerie Kinloch, whose work and love have long inspired us and who throws out the gauntlet with a bold administrative stance when few others stand up as courageously. Deep thanks for the privilege of learning from the incredible fellows of the National Council of Teachers of English's (NCTE) Cultivating New Voices Among Scholars of Color under the leadership of Valerie Kinloch and later Juan Guerra, and the teachers and teacher educators of NCTE's Professional Dyads and Culturally Relevant Teaching project, led by the ever-so-thoughtful Alicia Boardman and Bilal Polson.

Finally, thank you to Jan and Kelli Long for loving me like no one else and having my back every single day.

Preface

A Letter to Educators

Dear Colleagues,

We believe that teaching children to be proficient readers and writers has everything to do with teaching them to be knowledgeable and strong in their own heritage and self-worth while appreciating and standing up for the heritage and worth of those around them. It has everything to do with developing students' abilities to recognize injustices and use literacies to take action against them. This is at the heart of culturally relevant teaching—contradicting the dehumanization that takes place when histories, heritage, literacies, languages, family structures, and communities are marginalized, misrepresented, or omitted in classroom instruction; when Whiteness dominates curriculum and when students of color are underreferred to gifted programs, overreferred to special education, and inequitably disciplined; and when issues of justice are not taken up in curriculum in action-based ways.

Because most of us have grown up in systems that teach narrow views of what counts as normal, educational dehumanization can be difficult to see unless you are victimized by it. However, students receive messages that are crystal clear: They learn who matters as they witness which racial, ethnic, socioeconomic, religious, and gendered groups are normalized in curriculum and materials. They absorb perceptions about themselves and their peers when they observe who leaves the room for special needs and gifted programs, how families and communities are perceived, and how discipline practices are enforced. Throughout the school day, students internalize positive and negative biases about themselves and people around them. When they are not taught to critically question what they see, bias is reinforced in their hearts and minds. This matters in their school lives and in the future of the world.

We are two African American elementary school teacher-researchers (Carmen and Janice) and a European American university teacher-researcher (Susi) who worked together in Janice and Carmen's classrooms to better understand culturally relevant teaching. In this book, we share practices that have helped us address curricular omissions, marginalizations, and distortions while supporting students' literacy growth and development of a critical consciousness. Although we could write about many issues of educational omission and misrepresentation, we focus primarily on race and culturally relevant teaching. This comes from the concern that African and African American lives, histories, and strengths continue to be ignored, misrepresented, or relegated to the bottom of the priority list. We do not, however, see our practices as exclusive to African American children. We are concerned about the miseducation (Woodson, 1933) of all students as they internalize messages of White superiority because of the dominance of European and European American history, literature, sciences, arts, and so on in curricula and in tracking, discipline, and testing practices.

As we write, we hear teachers crying out, "But I don't discriminate; I love all my children!", "I certainly don't teach White supremacy!", or "We have standards; we have testing; they won't let me change the curriculum!" We hear you. We know the frustration of working within rigid mandates. We also know how it feels to love students and shockingly realize that many of our practices and policies contradict our expressions of love. We understand what it means to come face-to-face with the realization that any of us can be complicit in teaching Whiteness as superior even as we work toward change. But we also know the liberating feeling of coming to those realizations and then committing to pedagogical change in the company of caring colleagues.

This is what Carmen meant when she said, "We've been doing it your way long enough," the quote used in the title of this book. She captured the thinking of generations of educators cited throughout this book—educators who question the narrow center of schooling descended from the days of colonization. Her complete thought was, "We can no longer teach just according to the ways of the White, middle class. . . . You have to broaden your comfort zone and learn about lives and communities beyond what we've always been taught. We've been doing it your way long enough" (Long, Volk, Baines, & Tisdale, 2013, p. 2).

We invite you to join us in answering the call for change by choosing the culturally relevant classroom, which, as Janice says, begins with "seeing relevance in those who are sent messages of irrelevance every day." We offer support by sharing classroom examples and the voices of children and family and community members who also call for transformation. Their words make it clear that what we do in classrooms has an impact on raising new generations who will appreciate, support, and protect their own and one another's heritage, languages, beauty, brilliance, and the right to be safe in and proud of who they are—or are not. We also offer courage, purpose, and joy in the commitment to reenergized teaching that fills you up and pushes you forward because you know you are on the right side of change.

With love,
Janice, Carmen, Susi

Introduction
Knowing Us

"My whole theory of teaching had to redevelop." —Carmen

As teachers, our life stories are foundational to everything we believe, learn, teach, and the actions we take (or do not take) in and out of classrooms. For that reason, we introduce this book by sharing glimpses into the personal and professional experiences that led us to this work. Given the complexities of life's experiences, these narratives are, of course, partial. Their incompleteness means that further stories and questions linger in our minds and hearts. Thus, we offer them with gratitude for the children, families, and educators who keep us learning and growing well beyond the pages of this book.

JANICE

We lack so many things in the education system, especially teachers who understand what is missing and misguided in the teaching of Black children. Negative thoughts, stereotypes, and biases often influence how African American children are taught and treated. Lack of knowledge of our history keeps us locked into curricula focused primarily on European American heritage. This isn't good for any student.

I am fortunate that my family and my church filled many gaps for me. As an African American child, in spite of the White-focused curriculum at school, my home and church families never allowed me *not* to know African American heritage. They taught what schools did not. My Historically Black Church was a place of worship that was founded in the 1800s under a mulberry tree where African Americans came to worship and give one another courage for the long struggle. It brought history into my very being as my great-grandmother told stories of our people and we took trips in the area around our church to learn more.

My whole family got me reading about my heritage. They thought it was important to read school-assigned books like *The Diary of Anne Frank,* but they were also adamant that I be educated about change-makers from my own ancestry. For every book I was assigned at school about a White person, my family ensured that I read one about Black genius. My family kept up my self-esteem and heritage pride while school kept up the self-esteem of White children because everything they learned was about people who looked like them. When we learned about the past of my people in school, it started and ended with slavery, with a worksheet or two about Martin Luther King, Jr., and Rosa Parks thrown in for good measure.

My family also looked out for me by fighting for my identity as a conscientious, capable student. As much as my teachers said they loved me, their actions didn't always follow their words. They valued me as the quiet, sweet little girl who excelled, but only a few pushed me to the highest expectations, another form of discrimination and oppression. Home and community were the places where people really invested in me, listened to me, valued me, expected more out of me, and taught me.

My church and family teachers were the first people who encouraged me to teach, starting with Sunday school. It was as if they were thinking, "You start here and if you do a good job, we know you'll do a good job in the schools." My community prepared me, even though I didn't realize it at the time. So, today as a teacher, I'm held accountable not just to my students and our state, but to my people.

All of these experiences came together when I was an undergraduate at Benedict College taking two courses: Culturally Relevant Pedagogy with Dr. Gloria Boutte and Teaching the Black Child with Ms. Carrie Elliott. Also during that time, I met Susi. She came to learn from Dr. Boutte's forums on the education of African American students. Two years later, I met Susi again when we started a group to study culturally relevant teaching at the school where I was teaching. My background taught me that this was something that would benefit African American children, so I hopped right on it.

Our small group started meeting every other week. We read articles and looked at our district's pacing guides and standards to figure out how to meet requirements in culturally relevant ways. At first, I had a problem trusting Susi's motives in doing this work. People, especially White people, are always using children, particularly African American children, for experiments. I wanted to make sure that we were doing this work for the right reasons. I did not want to hand over information about my teaching or my children to someone who might not have the interests of African American children in mind. So, I watched how my students responded to Susi. I felt that if they were comfortable with her, then I would be fine.

I was also reassured because, in our study group meetings, we started by reading and talking about *The Dreamkeepers* (Ladson-Billings, 1994), which had been one of my favorite books at Benedict College. We watched videos like Adichie's (2009) *The Danger of the Single Story*. That really hit home because so many teachers create single stories about children and stick to them. As time passed, our relationship grew, and while we met as a study group after school, we also took the work into our classrooms.

My family taught me to never stop learning, so I also looked for ways to enhance my knowledge beyond our group. For example, the 2013 Black Education Congress that took place in Chicago gave me a stronger foundation and helped my identity evolve as a teacher who focuses on equity. The Congress was conceptualized by Dr. Iva Carruthers, Dr. Joyce King, Ms. Debra Watkins, Dr. Sam Anderson, Dr. Donald Smith, and "The Atlanta 45," a group of scholars dedicated to the education of the Black child. The congress had a powerful impact on my path of learning as I heard key leaders in Black education such as Dr. Anthony Browder, Dr. Geneva Smitherman, and Dr. Adelaide Sanford.

However, as I teach today, I keep going back to the most important teachers in my life—my home and church families. They are the people I try to model my teaching after. They give me the strength, knowledge, and courage to sustain a positive identity when other educational spaces do not. They keep my spirit from being crushed. I want to do that for my students.

CARMEN

I was always taught to have pride in myself and in the people I represent. That pride is not any less necessary today than it was years ago. I find myself constantly trying to instill this same sense of pride in my students because I see the opposite messages sent to me and many people of color. It has always been this way; the difference now is that we have social media to show everyone the inequities that Black folk have always known, the racial profiling and microaggressions we live with every day.

I recall incidents of racial profiling in my high school, but I imagine that many of my teachers, White friends, and administrators didn't notice them. I remember my White cheerleader friends saying negative things about Black people even when the other Black cheerleaders and I were standing right there with them. They would turn to us and say, "Well, we don't mean y'all. We like y'all." Then there was the White science teacher who told our class of predominantly African American students that we would never go to college. And there was the time when the assistant principal called a group of Black girls into the office for wearing shorts when the White girls who had worn shorts the day before had not been disciplined. This opened my eyes to what racism feels like. It let me know that there are different rules depending on race.

In terms of African American history, what I knew as I child, I learned from my father. Even teachers who might have wanted to teach Black history didn't because they didn't know it. Teachers still lack that knowledge today. My deeper education came as a college student at the University of South Carolina taking an elective course where I learned more about African American history, but there was nothing required in my teacher education program. After graduation, I learned more through informal gatherings where people would meet and teach each other about African history.

I definitely feel that desegregation, though it represented progress in some ways, also hurt us as a people. Much was taken away that has not been regained. Our Black teachers were often removed from our schools and White teachers replaced them, or we were sent to majority-White schools. This meant that we had teachers who did not know our communities, our history, or the toll that racism takes on us every day. They left our beauty and brilliance as African Americans out of the curriculum. Expectations were lowered because many teachers held negative stereotypes about what Black children can do.

All of these experiences were inside me when I took my first teaching job in my hometown. I accepted a job in the predominantly White, rural school. I thought the children needed to see a Black teacher. After that, I taught in California and Virginia and then returned to South Carolina, where I sought a job in a school with a predominantly Black student population. I wanted to work with our children but I knew I had to figure out a better way to teach. Many of the students were already labeled as "at risk" in 1st grade! Also, I was burned out because teaching felt repetitive and segmented. Nothing was meaningful. I had to redevelop my whole theory of teaching.

That's when I joined Susi and a group of other teachers at my school who were interested in working together to figure out culturally relevant literacy teaching. Susi and I had known each other for about 10 years. She was a professor in my preservice program and, with six other graduates, we wrote a book about our first years of teaching (Long et al., 2006). After I moved back to South Carolina, Susi began spending time in my classroom to get to know the children so we could think together about culturally relevant teaching.

From the first time I read about culturally relevant teaching, the ideas began to resonate. The more I read, the more I questioned my own teaching, and my desire to teach was reignited. Culturally relevant teaching gave meaning and joy to learning for my students, so it gave meaning and joy back to me.

I am committed to this work because I see my students prospering more than before, but also because it allows me to challenge racism that occurs when curriculum and materials focus primarily on Whiteness. This impacts families as well as teachers and children. One of the most validating comments I've heard came from the parent of a child I taught 5 years ago. She described the impact of my teaching on her own quest for knowledge about Black history: "Mrs. Tisdale, I feel like we have come full circle. You started us on this journey. You made me want to learn, too, and I have."

SUSI

Well into my adulthood, I was naïve about the reification of Whiteness, Christianity, and middle classness in schools and society. Although I couldn't have named it as such, I learned Whiteness as "normality" living in an all-White community, attending all-White schools, frequenting White-owned shops, participating in all-White extracurricular activities, observing all-White governmental leadership, and learning through White-dominated curricula. I grew up in systems that never questioned school celebrations of Christmas; making pilgrim hats and

Indian headdresses at Thanksgiving; teaching literature, art, and music of Europe as "high" art; and portrayals of most things African (if they were portrayed at all) as barbaric, exotic, or to be pitied. Even though my school years were in the midst of the civil rights movement, I remember no mention of it at school. And the only African American hero I remember learning about was Harriet Tubman.

Because "truths" about European rightness were so well taught, as a young teacher, I passed them on to new generations. I learned and repeated the Westward Ho!, Gold Rush, and *Little House on the Prairie* brand of American history. It never occurred to me to ask or to teach my students to ask: "Whose stories are told/untold?" "Who is telling these stories and what motives do they have to tell them this way?" "How might histories be differently told by African and Indigenous Peoples and their descendants?"

I came from a middle-class White household with many trappings of liberalism but little examination of structural discrimination. My father told stories about his college basketball team (in the 1940s) leaving a restaurant when their Black teammates were refused service, yet I had no idea about the racist practices that kept my neighborhoods White and the curriculum in my schools Eurocentric. I remember taking a copy of John Howard Griffin's (1961) *Black Like Me* to my 10th-grade social studies class. The book was passed around the room and came back with the words *N----- Lover* written on the title page. I remember thinking that my action pushed a racist peer to reveal her/himself. In actuality, it did nothing other than make me feel self-righteous. During high school, I tutored African American 1st-graders who lived in what was propagated by White-dominated media as the "inner city." I bought into a pitying mentality with no awareness of the rich histories, knowledge, and support systems that existed in the students' communities.

As a result, when I became a teacher, I was altruistic, not critical in my approach. While professing love for my Black students and an antiracist stance, I did not recognize racism in the way I followed along with negative stereotypes about my African American students and their communities. I contributed to the maintenance of a racist, exclusionary, privileging system.

My doctoral program at The Ohio State University was the first place I was introduced to the notion of criticality but without a focus on race. When I began teaching seminars in sociocultural theory, I *thought* I was focusing on race and racism but I was not. Any mention of issues of race was just that—superficial and safe, lacking criticality, depth, and honesty. My understandings began to gain depth as I worked with colleagues and doctoral students who are honored in this book's acknowledgments. They pushed (and continue to push) me to ask critical questions of myself and the institutions in which I work and play. I was ultimately drawn to equity pedagogies and culturally relevant teaching, and eventually to humanizing and decolonizing pedagogies.

Nine years ago, having known Carmen since her graduate program, I asked if I could work with her to figure out culturally relevant practices with her 1st-graders. Janice, who taught 1st grade down the hall, and two 2nd-grade teachers,

Valerie Collins and Stephanie Johnson, joined us. We met every other week in a little group we called Teaching for Excellence and Equity (TEE). We read, talked, planned, and tried out classroom practices. After a couple of years, Stephanie and Valerie moved on to other schools and we missed the opportunity to work with them on a daily basis. We give tribute to them here as our years together had a significant impact on what we were able to learn together. Indicative of their accomplishments, Valerie has moved into an administrative position and Stephanie recently received the Horace Mann Award for Teaching Excellence from the National Education Association.

The privilege of learning in the company of educators focused on social justice and the act of writing this book have pushed me to learn more, as do emboldened hate crimes, racial profiling, and microaggressions that have been long festering across our society. Yet, in spite of growth, I am reminded to be ever vigilant as I look back at my own microaggressive and complicit acts over the years: neglecting to call on the lone African American student in the back of my classroom, using the phrase "crack the whip" to urge students to work hard, assuming the African American man coming into my classroom in a white jumpsuit was the building's janitor, and on and on. With these experiences and the ongoing inequities in schooling and society, I see no other choice but to commit to standing up while continuing to learn with and from children, families, and colleagues.

INVITATION TO READ FURTHER

With our personal and professional narratives as a foundation, we invite you into our classroom stories. They are drawn from our work in Carmen and Janice's 1st-grade classrooms through Carmen's moves to 2nd grade, kindergarten, and 3rd grade; and as Janice moved from 1st grade to graduate school to after-school and summer programs to two different kindergarten settings. Their classes represented a range of diverse communities, although most years, their classes were either all African American children, or African American and European American students.

Reaching across these experiences, this book offers examples of how we strive to teach in culturally relevant, humanizing ways and includes thoughts on addressing standards, weekly pacing guides, and testing while challenging unjust systems of standardization and testing. Several chapters include "Continuing to Grow" sections to provide suggestions beyond those we tried in Janice and Carmen's classrooms. Text boxes can be found throughout the book suggesting children's books and professional resources. In Chapters 2 and 8, we provide support for self- and institutional examination, professional study, and taking steps toward institutional change.

As coauthors, the three of us use the word *we* when describing our collective voice. Otherwise, we name ourselves. Pseudonyms are used for children and family members. Community members' real names are used at their own request. We use the term *family members* instead of *parents* when we write about school–family relationships. We do this because the word *parents* privileges two-parent families when many students are beautifully supported by other adults in their lives: grandmothers, aunts, single fathers and mothers, and fictive kin (friends who are family in every sense of the word except biology).

Recognizing that no cultural, racial, or linguistic group is monolithic and that complex differences and commonalities exist within and across groups, we settled on a few terms to refer to racial and ethnic groups in this book. We move back and forth between the terms *African American* and *Black* when referring to persons who are of African descent living in the United States. We do this because both terms are used in the professional literature and by family and community members whose words illuminate issues throughout this book. To be consistent, we also move back and forth between the terms *European American* and *White* when indicating European descendants living in the United States. We use the term *Indigenous* when referring to original inhabitants of nations stolen by colonizers unless we are writing to focus specifically on Indigenous Peoples in the United States or Africa. Then we use the terms *Native Americans* and *Africans*. We capitalize the word *Peoples* in those contexts to emphasize the legitimacy of stolen nations (e.g., Inuit People, Navajo People, Wiradjuri People). We use *Latinx* to avoid the gendered terms *Latino* and *Latina*.

We offer this work to support educators in understanding the need to overhaul the current pedagogical norm. We share classroom practices not as recipes or formulas but as jumping-off points to spark ideas for teachers' own classrooms. We also write to administrators in hopes that they will commit to knowledge building so they can support, join, and applaud teachers' efforts. We see these commitments as one form of restorative justice in the work to correct and center that which has been invisibilized, marginalized, and/or distorted in policy and practice. We offer our thoughts in the interest of more honest and accurate systems of education that support students as players in the work toward an equitable society.

CHAPTER 1

Choosing Culturally Relevant Pedagogy

> As an approach deeply connected to teaching for social justice, culturally relevant teaching has long been an impetus for change we need in education. One reason is that many children receive the message that they do not matter—that their lives, communities, and histories are insignificant. They begin to believe that they bring nothing to the table, which means that other students learn that their lives matter more. The beauty of culturally relevant teaching is that we can send messages of humanity for all people while teaching children to read, write, and make a difference. —Carmen

In the 10 days between November 8 and 18, 2016, the Southern Poverty Law Center (2017) recorded 867 incidents of hate in the United States—and more than 1,800 by March 3, 2017. The majority were anti-Black and anti-immigrant. A third of these incidents took place in institutions of education; half of those were K–12 schools and were dominated by shouts from child to child: "Aren't you supposed to be in the back of the bus now?", "You will be deported," "Go back to Africa." Whites- and Colored-only signs were hung above a school's drinking fountain in Florida. "White Power" signs and nooses were hung in universities and schools. "Kill the n******s was written in a school bathroom. Chants of "Build the wall" (between the United States and Mexico) were directed at Latinx children in a California elementary school cafeteria and during a middle school volleyball game in Texas. Acts of anti-Black, anti-immigrant, antisemitic, and anti-Muslim violence included mosques vandalized, synagogues threatened, churches burned, and hijabs pulled from women's heads. More than half of the teachers surveyed reported an increase in racist and xenophobic acts in their schools. No state or region was immune.

This kind of discrimination is not, of course, isolated to this time period. In fact, these acts occurred not long after the 2016 United Nations Human Rights Council report on racism stated that "racial discrimination in the USA is alive and thriving" and that:

> Despite substantial changes since the end of the enforcement of Jim Crow and the fight for civil rights, ideology ensuring the domination of one group over another, continues

to negatively impact the civil, political, economic, social, and cultural rights of African Americans today. (para. 16)

This report fell on the heels of, and was informed by, the murders of Trayvon Martin, Philando Castile, Tanisha Anderson, Tamir Rice, Meagan Hockaday, Michael Brown, Aura Rosser, Alton Sterling, Eric Garner, Michelle Cusseaux, Walter Scott, and Freddie Gray, and the sanctioned brutalities against Sandra Bland, Dajerria Becton, Charles Kinsey, Breaion King, and Kalief Browder, to name a few. The report also reflected ongoing acts of racial and xenophobic profiling and microaggressions: African American shoppers regularly followed around shops under the erroneous assumption of wrongdoing, Latinx people screamed at for speaking Spanish, and countless persons of color brutally treated for nonexistent infractions or ill-founded suspicions (Guo & Vulchi, 2016).

In schools, parallel incidents of profiling occurred, such as the case of Ahmed, the Muslim middle school student who was taken away in handcuffs because teachers thought that his proudly constructed clock was a bomb; Shakara, an African American student violently treated for refusing to put down her cellphone; and Shakara's classmate Niya, who was arrested for filming the incident. Other cases include 6-year-old Salecia, who was handcuffed for an outburst at school and 6- and 7-year-old African American girls sent home because they wore puff ponytails or dreadlocks. Although in some cases steps are being taken to address so-called "unconscious" bias and the inhumane use of force, efforts are limited. This is clear as new incidents occur every day. A 2017 Maryland school district report documented an 80% rise in hate-based incidents that included scrawled messages such as "Brown people suck" and "Heil Hitler"; images of swastikas left on bathroom mirrors, a football field, and desks; Ku Klux Klan insignia carved into Halloween pumpkins; and nooses hung in educational institutions around the country. In the fall of 2017, the overtly racist and antisemitic acts committed in Charlottesville, VA, led to vocal denouncements of racist violence, and yet there continues to be little examination of how we arrived at and continue to live in a time of widespread racial profiling and xenophobia or what we can do to dismantle these "deadly patterns of racial violence" (Baker-Bell, Butler, & Johnson, 2017, p. 118).

So, what does this have to do with choosing the culturally relevant classroom? The answer is: *everything*. Not only do educators play an important role in raising the next generations of citizens who will respect and value themselves and one another (Asante, 2017), but we have a responsibility to do so by teaching against educational "spirit murdering," which Love (2016) describes as being just as deadly as murders in the streets. This includes the kind of overt profiling described in the paragraphs above but also the insidious academic, psychological, and emotional degradation and erasure that occurs when students' literacies, histories, heritage, and communities are marginalized, distorted, or ignored in the curriculum (Battiste, 2013); when institutional policies and practices lead to an under-referral of students of color to gifted programs (Ford, 2013) and overreferral to special-needs programs in what Blanchett (2009) calls "a resegregation of African American children" (p. 370); and when profiling and labeling occur as a result of inequitable assessment measures (Rosner, 2011) and unjust enforcement of discipline policies (U.S. Department of Education Office for Civil Rights, 2014).

In pockets of culturally relevant, sustaining, and humanizing teaching across the country, we see educators standing against this kind of devastation. They provide inspiration and hope. In the words of educator-activist Jamila Lyiscott (2017b), these are teachers who "do not let the fire defeat them" but use it as an opportunity to "sharpen [their] pedagogy." In this chapter, we explain why we join these educators to promote culturally relevant teaching as a pedagogical norm. Laying the groundwork for the practices shared in subsequent chapters, we focus on two fundamental discussions: (1) why we choose culturally relevant teaching and how we think about it, and (2) reasons why this book matters for every classroom.

CHOOSING AND DEFINING CULTURALLY RELEVANT PEDAGOGY

We are beholden to the past. We are shaping the present. We are responsible for the future. (James E. Wyatt describing the mission of Nannie Helen Burroughs, para. 10)

From the time of Anna Julia Cooper (1858–1964), Mary McLeod Bethune (1875–1955), Mary Church Terrell (1863–1954), and Nannie Helen Burroughs (1883–1961), the role of schools in challenging unjust societal norms has been clear. Each of these educator-activists took the stance that acts of bias and violence become ordinary when they are sanctioned through educational silence. One way in which silence occurs is through unquestioned curriculum that embraces narrow cultural, racial, and linguistic views of history, literature, art, languages, sciences, and so on. Learning within this norm, students come to see one group of people as the basis for the world's knowledge and others as peripheral, lesser than, or nonexistent. As a result, "countless youth, primarily of color . . . feel disassociated from, out of place in, and ignored within school space" (Kinloch, 2010, p. 176). When they are "dislocated culturally, socially, and psychologically" (Asante, 1992, p. 30), students of color are dehumanized and left without mirrors in which to see their potential (Bishop, 1990).

In contrast, the pedagogical dominance of Whiteness privileges White students with affirmation of their humanness through curricular mirrors of possibility and hope. This "unbalanced and incomplete education [means that they can easily develop an] overblown view of their place in the world" (Nieto, 2010, p. 25) as they are provided few windows through which they might appreciate the contributions, beauty, and strength of people of color. As a result, all students internalize positive and negative views of themselves and one another, ideologies that follow them into adulthood.

We see culturally relevant teaching as one way to address these issues because it requires teaching for the humanity of all people, particularly those who have been/are dehumanized through marginalization, suppression, or misrepresention (Salazar, 2013). Ladson-Billings's (1995a) original conceptualization of culturally relevant pedagogy asks us to embrace humanity by supporting students in three domains:

- Intellectual growth and academic success
- Cultural competence in students' own and other cultures
- The development of a critical consciousness

These are interdependent, not discrete, elements. Students in culturally relevant classrooms build proficiency in literacies, mathematics, science, and social studies while drawing on and building competence in their own and others' cultural communities and heritage. In turn, they use cultural knowledge and academic skills to "critique [and act against] current social inequities" (Ladson-Billings, 1995a, p. 477).

Broadening (Rewriting) the Curricular Center

The kind of teaching we are talking about requires educators to rewrite the curricular center by normalizing and correcting the histories, heritages, languages, and belief systems that have long been omitted, marginalized, or distorted. This means acknowledging that the curricula we teach today are little changed from those that were instituted during colonization. To justify enslavement, takeover, and genocide, European colonizers painted themselves as the holders of knowledge and virtue, and everyone else as uncivilized, barbarian, and less than human (Dunbar-Ortiz, 2014). This propaganda undergirded the educational practices developed to perpetuate it, thereby eliminating any possibility that European historians would provide accurate accounts of Indigenous Peoples' and their descendants' contributions to the world's knowledge (Battiste, 2013; Smith, 1999). This is the missing or distorted knowledge we work to re-write and re-center through culturally relevant teaching.

To visualize the need to re-center, it may be helpful to think back to Susi's reflection in this book's introduction. As a White student, every day of the year, Susi walked out of her K–12 classrooms knowing that her ancestors were not only "a part of the information" (Asante, 1992, p. 29), but they were the center of it. Her teachers did not have to use the words *White supremacy* to convey that the best of all knowledge came from people who looked like her. It was communicated through the dominance of Whiteness in the teaching of history, science, authors and artists, mathematicians, explorers, inventors, and world leaders. Asante (1992) called this the "white esteem curriculum" (p. 20). Nowhere in Susi's K–12 or undergraduate education was this questioned or challenged. It was and is the largely accepted curricular norm.

Thus, an important aspect of culturally relevant teaching is broadening the curricular center so that students are competent, knowledgeable about, and feel pride in their own heritage while centering, valuing, and committing to sustain the dignity, lives, and histories of everyone else (Paris & Alim, 2017). Key to maintaining this re-centering is not only developing students' cultural competence but also paying attention to Ladson-Billings's third tenet: equipping students with a critical consciousness. Discussed in detail in Chapter 7, this requires students to use knowledge from a broadened curricular center to identify further marginalizations, omissions, distortions, and injustices and take action to overturn them.

Defining the Work

Although the tenets of culturally relevant teaching provide guidance for our work, other pedagogies also speak powerfully to us. We are inspired and informed by culturally responsive (Gay, 2010), culturally sustaining (Paris, 2012), culturally revitalizing (McCarty & Lee, 2014), critical (Du Bois, 1903), assets and funds of knowledge–based (Gonzalez, Moll, & Amanti, 2005), critical race (Jennings & Lynn, 2005), reality (Emdin, 2016), equity (Banks & Banks, 2010), transformative (hooks, 1994), humanizing and emancipatory (Freire, 1970), decolonizing (Battiste, 2013), liberation literacies (Lyiscott, 2017c), Diaspora literacies (King & Swartz, 2016), healing (Baker-Bell, Stanbrough, & Everett, 2017), and revolutionary (Asante, 2017) pedagogies.

We choose the term culturally relevant pedagogy because, for us, it continues to speak in compelling ways. Janice reminds us that no other approach is viable without appreciating relevance. In other words, if we do not see relevance in the lives and histories that are most marginalized, we will not understand the need to decolonize our teaching, we will not give credence to the wisdom and knowledge of every student's family and community as pedagogical assets, we will be unable to recognize dehumanization in policy and practice, and we will not have the foundation needed to liberate, emancipate, or sustain relevance.

We agree with Paris and Alim (2017) that the word *relevance* has some drawbacks in that "it is quite possible to be relevant to something without ensuring its continuing and critical presence in students' repertoires of practice" (p. 5). We hope, however, that no matter what descriptors are used, the commitment to addressing systemic injustices and correcting, re-centering, and sustaining (normalizing) "the lifeways of communities who have been and continue to be damaged and erased through schooling" (p. 1) comes through loudly and clearly in the practices shared in this book.

Alert to corruptions. As we work to bring culturally relevant teaching to life, we see how easily educators' attempts can dissolve into corrupted versions of Ladson-Billings's (2014) original intent, so we try to remain alert to potential corruptions. For example, corruptions occur when attempts to build cultural competence dissolve into what Banks and Banks (2010) called a "tourist approach." This is the simplification and stereotyping of communities and cultures by merely "adding a few books about people of color, having a classroom Kwanzaa cele-bration, or posting 'diverse' images" (Ladson-Billings, 2014, p. 82), with little attention paid to cultural complexities that include histories of accomplishment, discrimination, and resistance. Corruption also occurs when the goal to promote academic success is co-opted to focus primarily on test scores and reading levels obtained through biased measures rather than on culturally relevant assessment of student growth and of students' ability to think and act critically. Finally, the goal to develop students' critical consciousness is corrupted when it is misperceived as engaging primarily in do-gooder actions like canned-good and clothing drives that can teach White-savior mentalities rather than develop students' abilities to identify institutional and individual injustices and take action toward change.

Taking up the call. With this in mind, we strive to take up the call to support children in developing cognitive, critical, academic, social, and global proficiencies through teaching that:

- *Anchors instruction in and normalizes complex historical and cultural knowledge* from perspectives that are missing from, marginalized, or misrepresented in current educational models (Au, Brown, & Calderón, 2016; Battiste, 2013);
- *Challenges* monocultural and monolingual practices and policies by *normalizing* "linguistic, literate, and cultural pluralism" (Paris & Alim, 2017, p. 93);
- Actively works to "*sustain and revitalize heritage practices* and deeply rooted community wisdom" (Dominguez, 2017, p. 225);
- *Embraces "cultural recombinations"* (Paris & Alim, 2017, p. 9) as students and teachers draw on home and community practices in conjunction with the conventions of schooling to reenvision teaching practice (Long, Volk, Baines, & Tisdale, 2013);
- *Expands notions of what counts* as print convention, text, literary genre, and language (Duncan-Andrade & Morrell, 2008); and
- *Teaches a critical stance* that equips teachers and students to recognize and challenge inequitable power dynamics and injustices using literacies to act against them (Cowhey, 2006; Vasquez, 2014).

Deepening the Work: Guided by African Cultural Principles

Our understanding of culturally relevant teaching continues to deepen as we embrace the call for praxis grounded in African cultural principles. This focus on "teaching for freedom" (King & Swartz, 2016) draws on principles originating in African tradition and influencing ethical thought around the world. Teaching according to these principles allows us to anchor our pedagogy in the very foundations of civilization (Diop, 1989; Hilliard, 1998), returning to a place of prominence histories that were denounced and degraded through mechanisms of enslavement and colonial empowerment. This anchor keeps us focused and purposeful as we strive to embody teaching that:

- Emphasizes a *collective humanity* and a *communal sense of belonging*, living the conviction that "there is no hierarchy of human worth that places some groups above others" (King & Swartz, 2016, p. 17);
- Builds curriculum by learning about and *centering knowledge from students' communities and histories*;
- *Accesses elders as wise mentors* and learns from the ways that families and communities support children's well-being;
- *Re-centers Indigenous voices* through accurate scholarship that informs teaching of history, literature, mathematics, science, literacy, and the arts; and
- Teaches students to *question knowledge* rather than just "recalling and reproducing it" (p. 17).

Committing to these principles challenges us to begin repaying the educational debt (Ladson-Billings, 2006) owed to every student by replacing narrow visions of what counts as knowledge, history, and humanity with strong and expansive culturally relevant teaching.

WHY DOES THIS BOOK MATTER FOR ALL TEACHERS?

Many of the examples in this book come from Janice's and Carmen's classrooms in schools where the populations were predominantly African American. We know that teachers with other demographics may ask what the book has to do with them. First, practices that normalize African and African American histories, heritage, and issues of discrimination and resistance are essential in every classroom if we are to re-center knowledge long missing from conventional curricula. Second, the practices shared in this book provide examples that can inform teachers of every demographic as we strive for culturally relevant teaching that (1) affirms humanity, (2) addresses the reality that children learn biases from an early age, (3) rejects essentialization and paternalization, (4) teaches within and beyond systems of standards and mandates, and (5) actualizes the equity-based goals of #BlackLivesMatter.

Affirming Humanity

Mr. Felder is a local barber and lifelong member of the community surrounding the school where we first worked together. Janice's 1st-graders interviewed him when they collected oral histories (Chapter 5). Several years later, Janice talked with him as he reflected on the state of schooling and humanity in general. He said:

Pride is something. You stick your chest out when you have pride. Knowing that your people have done so much makes you feel proud but *knowing that other people see my people as doing something good makes me feel good, too.*

Mr. Felder's words let every teacher know that, no matter the classroom demographic, each of us has a stake in raising the next generations who will or will not see themselves *and one another* as "doing something good." This is a part of the moral imperative that W. E. B. Du Bois (1903) entrusted to all teachers and that we accept when we commit to affirming humanity through culturally relevant teaching. Through this commitment, teachers promise to construct classrooms and curricula that are not merely inclusive of but that *center and normalize* ignored, tokenized, and misrepresented peoples, histories, and heritages.

To understand this as teaching for humanity, we draw on the concept of Ubuntu. Thought to have originated in southern Africa, Ubuntu philosophies are typically defined by the belief that we affirm our own humanity when we recognize "the humanity of others in its infinite variety" (Louw, 1998). We deny our own humanity when we deny the humanity of others (Hapanyengwi-Chemhuru & Makuvaza, 2014). Educators guided by Ubuntu know that when even one person or group of people is inaccurately depicted, tokenized, or invisibilized through practices and policies, humanity is withheld from every student.

Sometimes, however, in spite of loving intentions, educators may not recognize acts of dehumanization. At the same time, students readily absorb messages about who is humanized and who is not when they witness and experience:

- Classroom libraries and instructional texts dominated by Whiteness, English-only, and heteronormativity (Hughes-Hassel, Barkley, & Koehler, 2009);
- Teaching that omits, misrepresents, or tokenizes people of color and Indigenous communities rather than normalizing their histories, accomplishments, and languages daily in the curriculum (McCarty & Lee, 2014);
- A disproportionate number of students of color being referred for special education (Codrington & Fairchild, 2013) while White students are disproportionately referred for gifted classes (students of color are 50% less likely to be assigned to gifted programs even when their test scores are comparable to those of White students) (Ford, 2013);
- Children of color punished, suspended, and expelled more often than White students whose similar behaviors are more often ignored or justified (Gilliam, Maupin, Reyes, Accavitti, & Shic, 2016; Morris, 2016);
- Lower expectations held for students of color and higher expectations for White students (Gershenson, Holt, & Papageorge, 2016); and
- Two-parent, male/female family structures reified rather than normalizing the love, support, and strength in families cared for by grandmothers, aunts, fictive kin, single parents, and gay, lesbian, or transgender parents.

Challenging these practices that position some people outside "the bundle of life" (Tutu, 2011) and others at its center is a necessary entry point into culturally relevant teaching. The bottom line is that no teacher can claim to stand for humanity—and, in fact, we contribute to dehumanization—if we do not actively affirm and re-center voices, histories, and ways of being that are silenced, marginalized, or distorted.

Children Can Develop Racist Views from an Early Age

Along with our responsibility to affirm humanity is our responsibility to address the reality that children develop positive and negative biases about themselves and others from birth (Derman-Sparks & Edwards, 2010). This is another reason why we believe this book speaks to all teachers. Culturally relevant teachers recognize that children learn bias from an early age and teach actively against it, no matter the classroom demographic.

Regarding race, we know that children pay attention, from the time they are born, to ways that Whiteness is "consciously and unconsciously presented as a norm or a standard . . . in terms of appearance, beauty, language, [and] cultural practices" (Winkler, 2009, p. 3). This occurs in and out of school as students observe how people are or are not represented in books, songs, worksheets, magazines, food packages, faith-based texts, catalogs, billboards, television programming, and electronic applications (McCraw, 2014; Miller, 2015). Tatum (1997) calls this an unavoidable "smog in the air" (p. 6). We are surrounded by it day in and day out.

This conditioning to a belief in the superiority of Whiteness is affirmed by decades of research such as Kenneth and Mamie Clark's (1947) famous Black doll/White doll experiment, repeated with similar results 65 years later (Billante & Hadad, 2010; Davis, 2006). When given the choice between two dolls, 3- to 7-year-old White and Black children overwhelmingly expressed preference for the White doll as the pretty doll, the nice doll, the doll you want to play with. They regularly described the Black doll as the bad doll, the ugly doll. A range of studies has demonstrated that this racial bias is solidified in children as young as 36 months of age (Hirschfeld, 2008) and that, "by preschool years, children's comments [already] reveal misinformation about other racial groups" (Derman-Sparks & Ramsey, 2006, p. 51).

Erin Miller's award-winning study of her own three children illustrates this hidden curriculum—ways that White supremacy is learned even in a household priding itself on antiracist beliefs. Miller (2015) collected data for 9 months in many contexts of her White children's lives when they were 6, 7, and 10 years old. She delineated ways that the "insidious nature of racism" (p. 1) was learned through messages received at every turn:

> Normalized whiteness came through in a range of dominant discourses in the lives of my family through church and Sunday school, dance classes, magazines and catalogs

that came through our mail drop, worksheets and texts from school, the images on packages of food on our shelves, the toys with which my children played, and the very neighborhood in which we lived. Over and over they received messages about the supremacy of whiteness through an over-representation of white people and characters and the exaltation of white people again and again through portrayals of civic, patriotic, and leadership roles in our community. These messages were, quite literally, *everywhere* and they were sustained by simultaneous messages that conveyed systematic oppression and degradation of blackness . . . pictures of brown-skinned and helpless looking orphans on toy drive fliers that were routinely stuck in our mail. . . . Concurrently, there were also *discourses of omission* wherein the perspectives of persons of color were literally void in school curricula, neighborhood newsletters, daily mail, TV shows, songs on the radio, billboards, advertisements, and church bulletins. (p. 31)

Prior to Miller's (2015) study, she saw her children's upbringing as antiracist. She intentionally sought spaces for her children to engage in extracurricular activities with diverse groups of children, read Afrocentric literature, bought Black dolls, and introduced them to Latinx and Black artists and histories. And yet, every day the children received racist messages in and beyond their household. As Miller explained, "I know that most people genuinely strive to be anti-racist; yet the messages the children receive speak differently" (p. 45).

Just as insidiously, children of color—"victims of the same system" (Asante, 2017, p. 83)—receive and absorb messages that Whiteness equates to beauty, goodness, leadership, and intelligence. Coming from sites of authority, racist notions can become deeply internalized (Bevins, 2010) as children begin to believe messages about themselves. The resulting racial trauma is intense and can transcend generations with devastating impact on physical, emotional, behavioral, cognitive, and psychological health, and educational well-being (Caughy, O'Campo, & Mutaner, 2004).

We offer classroom stories in this book as an impetus for every teacher to "interrupt discourses of whiteness/racism" (Miller, 2015, p. 32). Miller reminds us that the work is not something we can entrust to a program, a month of the year, a lesson, or a teacher "here and there. . . . [It must be] systematically planned, explicit, and specifically focused" (p. 34), no matter the demographic of our classroom.

Rejecting Paternalism and Essentialization

Another reason we believe that this book speaks to every classroom has to do with our efforts to avoid essentialization and paternalization. Paternalization can be recognized in the dynamics that place some people in positions of subordination and others in places of power. We see paternalism, for example, when families are positioned as subordinate because of deficit views about them based on negative stereotypes.

Paternalization in this respect goes hand in hand with essentialization. Families and communities are essentialized when we hold stereotypical, one-dimensional, and therefore biased assumptions about cultural, racial, or socioeconomic groups (Brown & Brown, 2012) and use those assumptions to make judgments about families' and students' abilities. This also happens when we ignore the skillful ways that children blend knowledge from multiple cultural contexts to make sense of their worlds. Essentialized views fail to recognize this syncretic expertise (Long et al., 2013) as students integrate knowledge from home, community, and school to learn in "intersectional and dynamic ways" (Paris & Alim, 2017, p. 9).

An example of both essentialization and paternalization can be found in the work of educators such as Ruby Payne (2005). She erroneously categorizes—essentializes—students from low-income households according to characteristics such as "criminality, irresponsible parenting, and questionable morality" (Gorski, 2008, p. 137). Paternalistically, this stance disavows families' vast funds of community cultural wealth (Yosso, 2005), thereby positioning them as subordinate. This impedes the ability to teach in culturally relevant ways when educators are encouraged to believe that families have little to offer, so teachers may not seek the family and community knowledge that should undergird their teaching.

Through this book, we share practices that reject this kind of condescension. We tell stories about Janice and Carmen prioritizing families' voices and respecting families' wisdom as they plan for teaching. Through these stories, we illustrate ways that every teacher can reject essentialization and paternalization.

Standards, Pacing Guides, and Testing

We know that many teachers feel that their autonomy is compromised by standards and pacing guides. As a result, many do not attempt culturally relevant teaching. This means that students will continue to be either underserved or privileged by practices and policies that align with their histories, communities, and contemporary issues or invisibilize them.

Examples of culturally relevant teaching within and beyond standards are provided throughout this book. Janice and Carmen were required to demonstrate, in weekly lesson plans, exactly how they would address standards and specific indicators (skills). To meet these requirements, we planned culturally relevant lessons with the weekly pacing guide at our side, but we never let it lead, hinder, or constrain teaching. *We planned first to be culturally relevant* and then to address standards. In Chapter 8, we extend the standards conversation to discuss testing as well as strategies for beating the culturally irrelevant testing game while working to dismantle constraints that perpetuate histories of racism and exclusivity.

#BlackLivesMatter Matters in Every Classroom

It is morally imperative that a focus on African American histories, contributors, and sociopolitical issues should matter for all teachers. That does not mean that other lives are less important. Along with the founders of the #BlackLivesMatter movement (Khan-Cullors, Garza, & Tometi, 2016), we recognize and teach against tremendous societal and pedagogical inequities—"intersecting oppressions" (Collins, 2000, p. 138)—with regard to race, gender, sexual orientation, gender identification, language, ethnicity, religion, and body image. However, in this book, we focus primarily on African American and Indigenous African histories, contributions, and communities because we believe that a particular kind of restorative justice is necessary.

In addition to reasons outlined through this chapter, restorative justice is a necessary response to the ongoing portrayal and oppression of youth of color by "negative images and language" (Baker-Bell, Stanbrough, Everett, 2017, p. 132): Black males profiled as super predators (Johnson & Bryan, 2016), although statistics show that White males commit more drug-related crimes and mass murders than any other demographic (Alexander, 2012; Coates, 2015); Black women disproportionately criminalized, hypersexualized, or brutalized for nonexistent infractions or violations often dealt with differently when committed by White females (outdated license plates, burned-out tail lights, refusal to get out of the car or put down a cell phone) (Morris, 2016). These "distorted patterns of portrayals not only influence the public's understandings and attitudes toward Black youth but also how these youth view themselves and their communities" (Baker-Bell et al., 2017, p. 135).

Johnson and Bryan (2016) use the vivid imagery of bullets to draw parallels between the violently destructive nature of these societal realities and the bullets of silencing, disrespect, rejection, and omission that many students of color experience in schools. The metaphor of violence is echoed by North Carolina's 2014–2015 Teacher of the Year James E. Ford (2015), who spoke about the psychological and academic lynching of students as he asked teachers to consider "how much racism is kept alive both by what we teach and don't teach" impacting students of color *and* White students.

As a result of racial degradation, increasing numbers of families of color choose to homeschool their children. The National Home Education Research Institute reported that an estimated 220,000 families of color chose to homeschool in 2015 (Ray, 2015). Families cite factors such as the culture of low expectation for African American students (Mazama & Lundy, 2012), racial micro- and macroaggressions occurring in and out of the classroom (Haddix, 2016), and concerns for their children's sense of self-worth, history, and potential. Consequently, a sort of "racial protectionism" (Mazama & Lundy, 2012) is invoked as Black families seek experiences that will allow their children to build racial pride and positive views of self and heritage, "[un]willing to take any chances with their [children's] education" (Haddix, 2016, p. 18).

Homeschooling as a counterspace (Case & Hunter, 2012) provides support and sanctuary similar to that found in religious settings and community centers (Lytra, Volk, & Gregory, 2016), and Freedom Schools (Jackson & Howard, 2014). In many of these spaces, African American students learn academics, the nobility of their history, dignity of self and community, and strategies for thriving in a racist society.

The need for counterspaces is at the heart of the reasons why we believe this book matters for all teachers. If many African American children must rely on spaces outside of school to develop a sense of self-worth and learn about "Black excellence, Black achievement, Black culture, Black progress, Black possibility, Black appreciation, and Black expectation" (Kempner, 2015), and most White children do not learn, systematically and deeply, about Black genius and worth, *then we have a responsibility to do something about it in every classroom.*

As educational scholar Justin Coles put it, "every teacher needs to be aware of the anti-Blackness that exists in schools because it impacts the development of perspectives of every other child" (personal communication, February 23, 2017). It is something we must do as "restorative not only for African people, but for humanity at large" (Boutte, Johnson, Wynter-Hoyte, & Uyoata, 2017, p. 70). Thus, our focus on African and African American histories, heritage, and contributions is first and foremost *for* Black children and a love for them that is demonstrated in our teaching, no matter who sits in front of us in the classroom.

"NOBODY'S FREE UNTIL WE'RE ALL FREE"

In a 2016 documentary, Sonia Sanchez, one of the most important writers of the Black Arts Movement of the 1960s and 1970s, was quoted as saying that we can either maintain the status quo or acknowledge that "something's wrong [and] change it for the better" (Attie, Goldwater, & Gordon, 2016). As teachers, it is our privilege and responsibility to do just that by helping to raise new generations who will succeed because they feel strong in their own and each others' knowledge, history, and beauty, and are able to recognize inequities and work to challenge and overturn them.

Culturally relevant teaching can be at the heart of this work as we pull together for humanity, recognizing that dehumanization "marks not only those whose humanity has been stolen" (Freire, 1970, p. 26) but is a dehumanization of us all. We can be inspired and guided by educator-activist Fannie Lou Hamer (1971), whose words ring true through the decades reminding us that "Nobody's free until everybody's free" (para. 1).

CHAPTER 2

"Good Love"

Knowing Self, Knowing Families, Knowing Histories

His warm brown eyes greeted me at the door.

"Ms. Baines, my momma told me that she knows you!" I hesitated for a second. How did I know this child's family?

"I'm Jaleel Washington. You know my momma!" Then I remembered. Jaleel's older brother Derren arrived in my 1st-grade classroom 6 years earlier. That year, his mother and grandmother brought baby Jaleel to parent–teacher conferences. Derren was in danger of being held back, so his grandmother and mother and I worked together to help him gain the reading proficiency that allowed him to go on to 2nd grade. Greeting Jaleel on *his* first day of 1st grade, these memories came rushing back. "I do know you! Welcome to 1st grade, Jaleel!" —Janice

Janice's exchange with Jaleel lasted only a few seconds, but the moment was an important entrée for him into the rest of the year. He felt safe because a history of trust had been built with his family. His family knew Janice was someone they could count on, someone who respected them, viewed them as caring and capable, and shared their dedication to Derren. This history cradled Jaleel on his first day of school, so he greeted Janice with confidence. He knew Ms. Baines would believe in and take care of him.

Building this kind of mutually respectful, trusting, and supportive relationship did not happen overnight, and Janice's attitude and actions were critical to its success. She had deep respect for Jaleel and for Derren's mother and grandmother as wise elders in the children's lives. She demonstrated respect in the loving way she collaborated with them on the boys' behalf. She talked with and about them as caring experts in the children's education. Janice did not position herself as the all-knowing teacher but as a true partner in support of their children. She initiated the relationship by seeking *their* insights, taking her lead from them.

In addition, Janice demonstrated respect for the brilliance, beauty, and heritage of the children, their families, and communities. The minute they walked into her classroom, Jaleel, Derren, and their family could see prominent signs of how much they mattered in the history of the world and in the heart of their teacher. Children who were not African American could also see that their teacher honored Jaleel, Derren, and their histories in a classroom filled with books and posters about African American authors, scientists, world leaders, explorers, families, and communities; maps of Africa and the African Diaspora; and photos of the students and their communities as reference points for further learning. In other words, the open arms that greeted Jaleel reflected love that went far beyond mere proclamations of it.

In this chapter, we discuss these actions and attitudes as foundational to the kind of love that grounds culturally relevant teaching. We borrow Kiese Laymon's words, "good love" as Marc Lamont Hill (2016a) used the phrase to describe the uncompromising message that teachers will protect, learn from, invest in and believe in students and their families and communities. We see this love as anchored in teachers' commitment and responsibility to (1) *knowing themselves* through ongoing self and institutional examination; (2) *knowing families* by building trusting relationships, learning from family wisdom, and supporting families' rights in their children's education; and (3) *knowing histories* to be able to identify and replace curriculum, pedagogies, and practices that marginalize, distort, and invisibilize. This is the hard work that informs every other pedagogical decision. Without knowing self, families, and histories, what we do in the name of cultural relevance becomes another façade in a long line of attempts to create more equitable educational opportunities for every student.

KNOWING SELF

Teaching in this way is all about teacher attitude. We have to recognize that we may have biases that prevent us from seeing children and families' worth. But we often do not realize we are exhibiting a biased attitude because our ways feel normal to us. I'm sure I've been guilty of attitudes like that. So, we need to look at ourselves more honestly. If we don't, we hamper not only children's learning, but our own growth. —Carmen

Foundational to being able to teach in culturally relevant ways is the development of "cultural self-awareness and consciousness raising" (Gay, 2010, p. 70) and willingness to reflect "openly and deeply about cultural differences and racial inequities" (p. 72). Reality pedagogue Chris Emdin (2016) reminds us that "without teachers recognizing the biases they hold and how these biases impact the ways they see and teach students, there is no starting point" (p. 43). Sealey-Ruiz emphasized this in a 2017 interview as she talked about the importance of self-examination:

Teachers have to examine the self . . . particularly if you are a teacher whose backgrounds, languages, ways of knowing are different than your students'. . . . What are the implications of the cultural differences between you and your students? . . . How do you feel about a particular student if they are trans or if they are Muslim, Black, or if they are Haitian? The teacher has to do that type of self-reflective work. Once you do that, you begin to see your students in a very humane kind of way and advocacy just becomes natural.

Bias Can Be Hard to See

Because bias is so normalized, it can be difficult to see, particularly for those who are not victims of it. However, once we are alerted to its presence (see questions for self-reflection in text box), we have no choice but to work against it. The reality is that bias can be projected when we don't realize it. Remember Susi's description in this book's introduction of bias bubbling to the surface in microaggressive acts like not calling on the sole Black student sitting at the back of the class? Or think back to Chapter 1 and Erin Miller's (2015) children learning White superiority when she thought hers was an antiracist household. And consider findings from the 2016 Yale study of 135 preschool teachers revealing that the majority of them "held implicit bias that Black children were more likely [than White children] to exhibit challenging classroom behavior" (Gilliam et al., 2016, p. 12).

There are many ways we exhibit bias without realizing it. One way is by claiming colorblindness—"I don't see color"—as an antiracist stance, thinking we are "being fair by not seeing differences" (Ford, 2010, p. 32). In fact, claims of colorblindness perpetuate bias. Saying we are colorblind means closing our eyes to the marginalization, profiling, and stereotyping of people of color in historical accounts, popular media, literature, art, government, professional positions, school curriculum, on the streets, in shops, and on and on. If we "don't see color," we don't see or give credence to issues of power, privilege, and discrimination, nor to histories of contribution, strength, and resistance (Husband, 2016). Thus, colorblindness "protects Whiteness by maintaining the belief that race does not matter" (Castagno, 2014, p. 72), which in turn denies "the necessity to take action against racism" (Sue, 2015, p. 34) and against the Eurocentric nature of dominant pedagogies.

Another way bias is communicated is when educators devalue children's names. Comments like "Why can't they give their children American names?" reveal the bias that only certain names are acceptable, rather than celebrating the beauty of all names and their precious histories. Bias also occurs when educators mispronounce names or degrade the spelling of names, such as those with apostrophes like Ja'Quan (a practice that crosses national and cultural groups but is typically only demeaned when referring to the names of African American communities), and when children's family connections and heritage are erased by asking them to change from Miguel to Mike or from Anna Maria to Anne (Souto-Manning, 2007).

Bias can be projected with regard to one's own racial, cultural, or gendered group: women feeling that they should not be loud or dominant; multilingual parents in the United States feeling that they should speak only English with their children; or African Americans buying into colorism, the belief that there is greater beauty in lighter skin (Hunter, 2007). This is called internalized bias (internalized sexism, linguicism, racism): Members of oppressed groups are indoctrinated by dominant culture bias to believe negative views and stereotypes as truths about themselves and other people of their own ethnic, linguistic, or racial groups (Howard, 2010).

Teachers reflect these and other biases by adopting narratives, for example, that children from low-income and/or rural communities are not read to; Black boys are discipline problems; single parents from low-income communities don't care, support, or provide intellectual capital for their children; or that developing bilinguals have no language at home. We've all heard the deficit talk that reveals these biases: "*They* don't care," "*Those* families," "*That* neighborhood." Carmen talked about how easy it is to adopt biases and the need to be alert to them:

> I am African American and, although I teach in a school that is predominantly African American, I've learned deficit views that I had to address. Just being African American doesn't mean that I know or appreciate my students' worlds.

Mr. Felder, the neighborhood barber who grew up in the community surrounding Janice and Carmen's school, talked with Janice about the bias he sees every day:

> You would think that in 2015 this would be behind us, but we are still fighting the same thing that my generation had to fight. People might try their best to cover this up and say what I'm saying is not true but this is reality. I don't have to read a book on prejudice and bias. We have grown up and seen it and lived it firsthand. . . . I am surrounded by elementary and high school children that come in here and we talk. People say children don't want to learn, but that is not true. There are a lot of children who want to learn. . . . [Teachers] should be trying to lift them. You are dealing with human beings. [We] should be trying to lift up all of our children.

Institutional Bias

Merely engaging in self-examination, however, is not enough. In reflective and transformational work being done across the country, the examination of self is inseparable from the examination of institutions (Nieto, 2017). For educators, this means looking for bias, privilege, and oppression in the institutions of schooling: curriculum, standards, book collections, program adoption, discipline enforcement, language policies, assessment measures, identification of students for special-needs and gifted programs, and hiring and zoning practices. Schools engaged in self-study examine these institutions to identify, dismantle, and replace practices and policies "that systematically reflect and produce racial inequities" (Boutte, 2016, p. 36). Carmen described examples from her own observations of institutional racism as "alive and well in our schools and classrooms":

EXAMINING SELF

- What are my assumptions about and expectations for students of color, immigrant students, students from low-income households, and their families?
- What knowledge and expertise do my students and their families bring to my classroom? Do I recognize and utilize that knowledge and their brilliance? If so, how? If not, why not?
- Do I use deficit- or assets-based language when thinking and talking about students and their families? Do I hear it from colleagues and administrators? How do I react in ways that lead to change?
- What can I learn by video-recording my teaching to reflect on who I call on most and least frequently? Who do I position as smart, beautiful, dependable? How do I do that? Who is disciplined the most and the least? Are there demographic patterns in these observations? What can I do to change that?
- How do I make decisions about who I will refer to special education or gifted programs? What are the demographics of each?
- See Chapter 8 for further support for self-examination.

I see it when a White teacher tells me not to fight to get a Black boy out of special education because "It will be too hard to get him back in." I see it when school lines are drawn to fit what a certain group wants for their children. I see it when most of the books provided for reading instruction depict children who don't look like my students and when assessment materials have nothing to do with anything my students can connect to.

Susi provides an example from her own experiences with institutional bias. It comes from a meeting with administrators who were discussing a school with a predominantly African American population from low-income households. One of the group members said, "Most of these children come to school nonverbal." Of course, the students were *not* nonverbal; however, this view is often derived from highly refuted research that has been adopted in many places as an institutional "truth." The research suggests that children from low-income homes speak significantly fewer words and are therefore less ready for school than children from middle- and upper-class homes (Hart & Risley, 2003). Though denounced by language scholars (Dudley-Marling & Lucas, 2009) for its language prejudices and the inaccurate correlation between the amount of words one speaks and school readiness, the study has been "hugely influential in driving policy and practice" (Kinard, Gainer, & Huerta, 2018, p. 112). This is an example of how flawed research can inform institutional bias.

Insidiously, these biases seep into our portraits of children and families, resulting in deficit labels that seriously impact our expectations and ability to teach well. Kirkland (2016b) talks about this as "the biggest interruption to culturally relevant teaching." Thus, our attention to self- and institutional examination is essential.

Without examining whether or not our curricula, words, actions, policies, and practices are consistent with our declarations to embrace diversity, we can contradict our promises to teach for equity.

But I'm Not Racist! The Courage to Engage

Most of us see ourselves as "good, moral, and fair-minded human beings who actively stand against overt acts of discrimination" (Sue, 2015, p. 31). We tend to think of racism only as extreme expressions—"water hoses, lynchings, racial epithets . . . [and not how it] is embedded in the structures of a social system" (Alexander, 2012, p. 183). So, when we are asked to examine ourselves, particularly around issues of race, feelings of defensiveness are understandable. Most White people have been socialized *not* to recognize White dominance masquerading as normality. As a result, when confronted with the notion that we may harbor racial bias, a kind of upheaval is experienced that James Baldwin (1962) described as "terrifying because it so profoundly attacks one's sense of one's own reality" (p. 9). As a result, we become experts at deflecting, avoiding, or denying stories of discrimination: "I didn't really mean it that way"; "He's just being too sensitive"; "She's always pulling the race card."

Thus, examining ourselves and our institutions requires a kind of courage and willingness to be vulnerable and step back from any kind of defensive posture. In her 2016 book, *Educating African American Students,* Boutte guides us to recognize and negotiate triggers that may keep us from engaging in thoughtful examination of self. She helps us take a breath when defensive feelings rise, reminding us of our commitment, which is, of course, to the well-being of every child. Janice's words cut to the chase as we consider this step we all must take:

> It hurts me to the core when teachers don't want to examine these things. We must talk about it. We have to knock out the biases that we may have toward people. Sometimes that means leaving our comfort zone. Are we going to stick with our comfort zone or are we going to broaden it so we can really teach?

What Do We Do?

The need for self- and institutional examination grows out of what Joyce King (1991) calls "dysconsciousness" or an uncritical habit of mind. We can develop a *critical habit of mind* by routinely engaging in self- and institutional examination during grade-level and faculty meetings, professional development sessions, preservice teacher education programs, and individual reflections. We hope the questions and resources posed in this chapter's text boxes will be helpful in that process. Through the rest of this book, we suggest next steps—moving from reflection to action so that our examinations are not merely "performative" (Dominguez, 2017, p. 231) but focused on the transformation of practice and policy.

EXAMINING INSTITUTIONS

Looking carefully at the following institutions in my classroom, school, and district, what elements of bias do I discern as I consider oppression and privilege: Where do I see omission, marginalization, over- and under-representation, tokenization, and misrepresentation? Is change needed? What kind of change? How will I ensure that change occurs?

- Curriculum?
- Books and materials?
- Pacing guides?
- Discipline policies and enforcement?
- Academic referrals (special education and gifted programs?)
- Daily practices?
- Individualized Educational Program (IEP) meetings? Response to Intervention (RTI) meetings?
- The walls of hallways, front office, classrooms?
- Attitudes and practices involving families?
- Language used to describe and label students and families?

See Chapter 8 for further support for institutional examination.

RESOURCES TO SUPPORT SELF- AND INSTITUTIONAL EXAMINATION

Alexander, M. (2012). *The New Jim Crow*
Baldwin, J. (2017). *I Am Not Your Negro*
Boutte, G. (2016). *Educating African American Students*
Castagno, A. E. (2014). *Educated in Whiteness: Good Intentions and Diversity in Schools*
Coates, T. (2015). *Between the World and Me*
Du Bois, W. E. B. (1903). *The Souls of Black Folk*
Howard, T. (2014). *Black Male(d): Peril and Promise in the Education of African American Males*
Jensen, R. (2005). *The Heart of Whiteness*
King, J. & Swartz, E. (2016).*The Afrocentric Praxis of Teaching for Freedom*
Milner, R. (2015). *Rac(e)ing to Class*
Morris, M. (2016). *Pushout: The Criminalization of Black Girls in Schools*
Pollock, M. (2008). *Everyday Antiracism: Getting Real About Race in Schools*
Sue, D. W. (2016). *Race Talk and the Conspiracy of Silence*
Woodson, C. G. (1933). *The Miseducation of the Negro*

KNOWING FAMILIES

> You loved my babies and my family like we were your own. That's a beautiful
> thing about the teachers here. Thank y'all for helping mold my baby. —Ms.
> Sims, 1st grader Sameka's mother

Ms. Sims clearly felt a sense of belonging as the parent of a child in Janice's 1st-grade class, as did Derren and Jaleel's family who were introduced at the opening of this chapter. Building mutually supportive relationships with families is an essential anchor in the commitment to "good love" that grounds culturally relevant teaching. In our experiences, we've found that those relationships center on (1) building trust, (2) engaging in home visits that connect rather than condescend, (3) getting to know the community, and (4) supporting families' right to be heard and respected.

Building Trust

Building trusting relationships with families, particularly when family members may have received messages that they are not good enough (Myers, 2013), takes genuine humility and commitment on the part of teachers and administrators (Long, Souto-Manning, & Vasquez, 2016). We share two examples to illustrate actions and attitudes that we found to be fundamental in building trust.

Jordan. Jordan was a 1st-grader in Janice's class. He always talked about his grandmother, Ms. Thomas. Recognizing their special relationship, Janice knew it was important to reach out to Ms. Thomas when she began to have concerns about Jordan:

> Jordan had a hard time with school and wasn't attending regularly, so I
> had to reach out, not just to his mother, but to his grandmother because
> his mother was often sick. I called his grandmother and she filled me in on
> Jordan's mother's illness. That was the start of our relationship.

After Janice reached out to her, Ms. Thomas began walking Jordan and his siblings to school every day and Janice talked to her every morning. Janice explained how, in the process, they learned from each other:

> [Jordan's grandmother] had a way with him that was so powerful. One way
> was that she allowed him to have ownership of his learning, by showing
> him his own abilities. Sometimes, she would act like she didn't know a word
> or know how to read something. That motivated him to read it to her, and
> showed him that he could be the expert, so I started using that strategy, too.

Janice sought Ms. Thomas's wisdom and used it. In return, Ms. Thomas trusted and reached out to Janice, often saying, "Ms. Baines, tell me what I need to do." Janice saw a transformation in Jordan's motivation at school. He would say,

"[My grandma] told me you called her" or "Ms. Baines, I'm gonna read this book to you because we practiced last night." This trusting connection also meant that Janice and Ms. Thomas were able to talk *together* at the end of the year to make the decision that Jordan should spend another year in 1st grade and that he should stay with Janice. His grandmother said, "Ms. Baines, he started with you, he's going to finish with you."

Elements of this relationship are fundamental to trust and culturally relevant teaching. First, Janice never questioned Ms. Thomas's credibility; she placed Ms. Thomas's insights about Jordan at the center of their relationship. From their first interaction, Janice respected Ms. Thomas as knowledgeable in Jordan's life. Second, Janice persevered—she did not moralize or give up when Jordan's mother could not come to school; she searched until she found out more about the situation and recognized that all kinds of family networks can be supportive. In Jordan's case, the primary support came from his grandmother, but it could have come just as effectively from a father or mother, cousin, neighbor, or family friend. Third, Janice and Ms. Thomas developed a relationship that was reciprocal. Janice respected Ms. Thomas's wisdom and learned from her. Without that relationship, Janice could have gone through the entire year unable to support Jordan and she would have missed insights that enriched her teaching for years to come.

Zaire. Another example of building trust comes from a year when Carmen taught kindergarten. Five-year-old Zaire's godmother, Ms. Jackson, was frustrated by the reward and punishment system being used—a behavior chart on which the school's intervention team suggested that Carmen post stickers when Zaire exhibited "good" behaviors (sitting quietly, doing his work) and remove him from classroom when he exhibited "undesired" behaviors (running around the class, for example).

Ms. Jackson voiced her objections: "We can't just keep giving him a chart and casting him out of the classroom." Carmen agreed. She knew it was important to consider whether or not other issues may have led to Zaire's behaviors, such as deficit attitudes she may have unwittingly conveyed; his cognitive need to be challenged and engaged; his physical need to move around; and his own life, issues, and interests (Noguera, 2014).

Carmen and Ms. Jackson were well aware that actions taken in the early years can create profiles that criminalize students from a young age, creating labels that are almost impossible to shed as children continue through school and into their adult lives. They also knew that negative profiles easily become self-fulfilling prophecies as children start to believe the characteristics imposed on them, potentially pushing students into the school-to-prison pipeline (Howard, 2010).

Trusting the wisdom in Ms. Jackson's words, Carmen explained the importance of her own self-reflection as she stepped back from what could have been a defensive reaction:

She may sound hostile to some people but she is fighting for her child *and* she is bringing knowledge that the rest of us don't have. Rather than thinking,

"How can she talk like that?," I have to ask what I can do differently. I need to let her know that I hear her and respect her thoughts. She's worried about her child getting a label and being put out of the classroom where he won't be learning. She's right. So, we have to figure out how to fix it.

In the weeks that followed, Carmen's actions reflected her commitment to recognizing Black males' "strengths, promise, and potential" (Howard, 2014, p. 19). She put away the sticker system and relied instead on deepening her relationship with Zaire and his godmother. She found out that he was close to his grandfather, who was very ill at the time. Carmen spent more time talking with Zaire and letting him know she was there for him. She worked on helping him see—through the work he produced and his positive contributions in class—that he had much to offer and did not need a chart to tell him what to do, that he was actually in control of his own behavior.

Carmen also instituted what she called an All-Male Reading Blitz through which African American men from the local community—lawyers, sports figures, businessmen, governmental leaders—read to the children, providing examples of strong role models. They also held conversation sessions so the boys could build relationships with professionals and be supported as brothers. Carmen watched her male students' confidence grow because, as the boys said, so many "important men" came to spend time with them. At a time when schooling and society often positioned Black males with a kind of nobodyness (Hill, 2016b), Carmen wanted her students to know that they were somebodies, already filled with greatness. The students' sense of purpose matured through the mentorships, which led to long-term mentoring relationships. Illustrated in examples throughout this book, Carmen also instituted a curriculum that let Zaire know that he mattered in the history of the world. All of this helped deepen trusting relationships with families like Zaire's, who saw Carmen taking constructive steps toward believing in and supporting their children.

Home Visits That Connect Rather Than Condescend

Much can be learned and relationships can be built by getting to know families on their own turf. Janice and Carmen made a point of spending time in students' homes, not as voyeurs, but as learning/teaching partners ready to build relationships and learn from the wisdom and experience of family members (López-Robertson, Long, & Turner-Nash, 2010). Carmen recommends initiating visits with a simple phone call that sets the tone: "I'm excited to have Damion in my class this fall. I'd love to come to visit any place that you would like to meet so you can get to know me and I can get to know you."

During the visits, Janice and Carmen asked how the children learned best and what strategies families used to teach their children about anything from reading to bicycle riding to fixing breakfast. Then they used that knowledge to inform their teaching.

Visits to students' homes quickly became a favorite aspect of getting to know them. Invisible walls started to come down just by meeting in a setting where families felt comfortable.

Carmen remembered one of her first visits. It was to the home of 1st-grader Marcus:

> Marcus's grandmother, Ms. Scott, welcomed me into her home with a big smile. She lived in a housing area near the school. Marcus's face lit up once he saw me. I could see in his eyes that it meant everything to have his teacher in his home. I hadn't expected to stay long; however, as laughter and kinship entered the room, the time went by quickly. Marcus's grandmother shared a lot. She showed me pictures of family she had on display and gave me the history behind each of them. We made a bond that continued after Marcus left my classroom. I soon became a staple in the neighborhood with visits to other students' homes. The neighborhood knew me and it felt good to be known.

Challenging deficit assumptions. Overturning deficit views—"one of the most prevalent forms of contemporary racism in U.S. schools" (Yosso, 2005, p. 75)—can be an important outcome of home visits if they are initiated with a willingness to recognize and respect families' knowledge. Susi talks about the courage of teachers with whom she has worked who faced up to their own negative assumptions after spending time in homes and communities. In one example, a European American literacy coach (Becky) initially bought into deficit assumptions propagated by the school and society about Black children from low-income households. She assumed that 3rd grader Jonathon "because he was Black . . . had not lived with his mother in the projects, had no regular routines in his life, his father might or might not be a part of this life, his family lacked literacy skills and were poorly educated" (Long, Anderson, Clark, & McCraw, 2008, p. 264). Jonathon was also profiled as hyperactive and as a student who couldn't or wouldn't memorize his spelling words each week. His mother was described as uncaring because she didn't come to parent-teacher conferences. Tearing down these perceptions, Becky's experiences with the family at home and at church revealed Jonathon's expertise in memorizing Bible verses each Sunday and sitting with no evidence of hyperactivity during his grandmother's choir practice. His "uncaring" mother was, in fact, deeply caring. She helped him with homework, listened to music with him, and took him to work with her in the church's soup kitchen. This recognition was critical to her ability to teach Jonathon as she confronted her own biases—"The ones I didn't think I had":

> I was very fond of Jonathon, how could I have bias? But I was wrong about so many things. This leads me to believe that there is a lot of assuming going on in classrooms and that those assumptions can be blinders that keep us from seeing what is really there. (p. 266)

Learning about literacy proficiencies. In Janice and Carmen's experiences, home visits also provided opportunities to learn about and highlight children's literacy proficiencies (Gregory, Long, & Volk, 2004). They were able to point out literacy resources everywhere: "You have *Ebony* magazine, you have the Bible, you have playing cards, cereal boxes, soda cans. Let's talk about how you can use these things to support your child as a reader." Naming the wealth of proficiencies that children displayed at home, Janice and Carmen helped families recognize and build on their children's expertise and, at the same time, they learned about literacies they could bring into the classroom as teaching/learning texts and to broaden definitions of what counts as literacy (see classroom examples in Chapters 3 and 4).

Hesitance. When teachers are hesitant to spend time in students' homes and communities, Carmen's advice is to take the focus off yourself and consider how families might feel. She reminds us that "even though someone's house might not look like yours, remember that it's somebody's home, and this is somebody's family."

The reality is that families may also be skeptical and fearful, often with good reason. They may be accustomed to teachers or social workers exhibiting condescending attitudes or making judgments based on uninformed assumptions. Carmen described how being a presence in the community and following a mother's lead led to insights about why 1st-grader Ileka's mother had been hesitant to make contact:

> I had just visited Marcus's grandmother and I was walking by Ileka's apartment a few doors down. I had tried unsuccessfully to set up a visit, but Ileka's mother happened to be standing in the doorway so I asked if I could talk to her. We talked right there in the doorway. She was guarded at first. However, the longer we talked, a certain ease came into the conversation. She shared with me that she had been in special education when she was in school. She was afraid Ileka was like her. She talked about how she was trying to help Ileka but didn't know what to do.

This breakthrough was important for Carmen in understanding why Ileka's mother may have avoided setting up a visit or coming to school. Perhaps she was fearful based on negative memories of her own schooling or, having received messages of condescension in the past, had lost confidence in her ability to help her daughter.

Janice suggests flipping the script when teachers are reticent or fearful by considering how families might feel on your turf. Parallels to how she sometimes feels in White communities puts it all in perspective:

> It doesn't take much to learn how frightening and dangerous it is to be a person of color in this country—profiled when walking down the street,

driving a car, shopping in a store, playing with a toy gun. . . . When you're the only Black face, it's frightening knowing that you could be profiled and taken down just for walking there. So you worry about going out of your comfort zone? Turn it around. Just go.

Get to Know the Community

Knowing families also means knowing the communities in which they live, which requires "ventur[ing] out of the school and into everyday life" (Wyman & Kashatok, 2008, p. 300). A much-loved community elder, Ms. Myers, offered similar guidance. Having worked in Janice and Carmen's school for many years, she had observed countless teacher–child–family relationships. She advised teachers: "Go to programs that the kids are involved in outside of the school. Go see what they do in church—what they are learning so you get a better understanding of where they're coming from."

Access. Carmen and Janice gained access to community settings through their relationships with the children. For example, on Wednesday mornings, many of Janice's students came with stories of Tuesday night church events and often invited her to attend. Janice's participation in church functions brought her closer to the children and families. She learned about people who held the children in high regard as well as ways her students used literacies in spaces that were important to them (McMillon & Edwards, 2000). Janice's story about Jabari provides an example of how taking time to listen to children at school can lead to experiences within the community:

> My little Jabari, he always went to Bible study and I would say, "Listen well so you can tell me the story tomorrow" so he had to listen and learn to be able to tell me about it. One day, he said, "You could come, Ms. Baines." I said, "Okay" and told him I would come the next week. That week, he remembered, "Ms. Baines, this is your week!" Many of the children were there. It was like I was a movie star. They were calling out, "Ms. Baines! Ms. Baines!"

Community members who worked in the school—custodians, teaching assistants, administrators, other teachers—also helped us learn more about and gain access to the surrounding neighborhoods. We sought those who did not repeat media-promoted deficit narratives of low-income Black communities but who saw the richness of the community and loved and respected it. Janice and Carmen made it their business to get to know owners of small businesses: grocery stores, barbershops, restaurants, day care centers, and other establishments frequented by their students. Susi got to know people at the local clinic and wellness center. Meeting one community member led to another and another as we learned more about the historic neighborhoods in which the school was situated. This laid the groundwork for oral histories the children would ultimately collect (Chapter 5) while helping us locate students within their communities' strengths, history, and heritage (King & Swartz, 2016).

No more drive-throughs. Our experiences getting to know communities were a far cry from the "drive-throughs" that are increasingly instituted by schools—loading teachers onto buses and driving them through local communities. The purpose of these "tours" is ostensibly to get to "know where students are coming from [and to] . . . get a feel for the people" (ColaDaily, 2016). However, these ventures can easily "do more harm than good" (Milner, 2015, p. 41) as they become superficial and voyeuristic. The practice commodifies families as teachers peer out the bus windows, reflecting the presumption that it is ethical for one group of people to make distanced judgments about another.

Although some tours include stops at local places of worship and community centers, they rarely have much to do with actually getting to know people, which means that stereotypes can be "reinforced rather than dispelled" (Milner, 2015, p. 41). There is still a kind of cruise ship mentality—get off, walk around, talk to a few people, and get back on the ship. W. E. B. Du Bois (1903) called this "car window sociology"—seeking to understand a group of people by "devoting a few leisure hours . . . to unraveling the snarl of centuries" (p. 94) while professing to have insight about a community's cultural wealth and its complex history and challenges.

Hearing and Respecting Families' Insights

Critical to knowing families was learning to be their allies. To do this, Janice and Carmen supported families in sharing their insights about their children. This was not always easy. Trust had often been eroded because families had experienced degradation when their methods of support had not been recognized or valued in previous school experiences. We know this from our own experiences but also from research like Michele Myers's (2013), which revealed clear differences between teachers' definitions of support and ways that families in low-income, rural, Black communities effectively supported their children. Myers, who was the school principal, often heard teachers "blame a child's academic failures on what they believe is a lack of care, concern, and involvement by a child's family" (p. 43). In reality, the families supported students in a rich variety of ways: They accessed experts within family networks to help children with academic content, took their children to the local library and sporting and musical events, impressed on children the importance of doing their best, and taught their children the racialized reality of having to look twice as tidy and behave twice as respectfully to be seen as having the academic potential of their White peers.

Given the reality that teachers may not recognize or give credence to this kind of support, it is not surprising that families avoid schools and feel that their voices are not welcome. Carmen noticed this in her own classroom:

I ask parents to tell me what their concerns are, but sometimes they don't say anything because history has taught them that they don't really have a voice anyway. Some parents have received the message that they don't have much to bring to the table, that they don't have value in their child's education. So they don't speak out.

IEP (individualized education program) and RTI (response to intervention) meetings are examples of spaces where this can be evidenced. These sessions typically involve school-based personnel meeting with family members to draw up a plan for a child identified as having academic or behavioral issues. In our experience, letters requesting parental presence rarely affirmed families as experts in their children's education or as major contributors to the meeting. Carmen explained:

> They just get a letter that basically says your child has a behavior problem or is below grade level academically, so it stands to reason that family members would come to meetings holding back, embarrassed, or uncomfortable. You're already coming with a sense of insecurity.

Recognizing this, Carmen and Janice make a point of talking to families prior to the meetings "to explain what the real deal is." They let family members know that personnel may do a lot of the talking, but that families have a right to be the dominant voice. Carmen tells parents: "You can make things change. When you know something's not right, you can say something. Bring it to the table."

Even with Janice and Carmen's good intentions, however, history and the hierarchical atmosphere of these meetings can result in further family alienation. Merely telling families to use their voices is very different from intentionally centering their voices and making it comfortable for families to use them. This was clear when Ms. Jackson, Zaire's godmother, was asked to meet with the school's intervention team. After the meeting, Ms. Jackson told Carmen that she had felt unsupported. She was keenly aware that school personnel around the table made little eye contact with her, talked over her, or tried to pacify her, and that a key administrator sat typing on an iPad without speaking. The one-sided nature of the session gave her the feeling that no matter what anyone said, the motives were disingenuous. She even felt that Carmen, who nodded in agreement with Ms. Jackson during the meeting, was condescending: "You don't have to show me that you agree with me. I don't need that."

We see a few issues at play here. First, Ms. Jackson received messages that her views were not sought or respected. This was clear in the administrator's preoccupation with her iPad and others' lack of eye contact. Second, a prior history of condescension and the lack of validation was likely so strong that Carmen's head-nodding was experienced as paternalization, particularly when it was not paired with actual changes to the school-dominated format of the meeting. Finally, even though Carmen had explained "the real deal" to prepare Ms. Jackson for the meeting, there was no preparation of school personnel to change the dynamic

---

LEARNING FROM FAMILIES

- How can you learn from the wisdom, knowledge, literacies, languages, and support in students' families and communities by getting to know them where *they* feel safest and most confident?
- How can you demonstrate your belief in families as credible, wise, and knowledgeable, placing their insights at the center of your relationship?
- How will you persevere in connecting with families even if it seems like you are getting no response?
- In what ways will you privilege family and community knowledge as you reflect on children, their abilities, and your curriculum?
- How will you alter the nature of meetings to put families in the driver's seat in nonthreatening ways?

---

that positioned Ms. Jackson as subordinate. Acknowledging the wisdom of family members (Boutte, 2016), and allowing families to set the purpose, tone, and pace, can make all the difference in the outcome of meetings like this (Luján, 2016). As Janice says, "Remember that you may have a degree in education, but you don't have a degree in someone else's child."

KNOWING HISTORIES

> It would've been different if the focus wouldn't have been just on White people. Then when I had my children, I could have taught them about Black people. So instead, I've taught them about more White people because that's what I was taught. —Ms. Willis, 1st grader James's mother

Hand in hand with knowing self and knowing families, good love in culturally relevant classrooms means committing to unlearning and relearning histories. As introduced in Chapter 1, this requires rewriting curricula to center that which has been stolen, mistold, and marginalized. Family members like Ms. Willis (above) help us understand why this is so important, as do students like Alex, who told Carmen that if we don't change what we teach, "everyone will think it's all about White people and this is the way we are supposed to live."

Ngũgĩ wa Thiong'o (2005) wrote that this kind of change involves a "decolonization of the mind" (p. 4). This means investing *re-membering*, or putting back together the "once-connected strands [of silenced histories] that have been pulled apart" (King and Swartz, 2014, p. 16). Dillard (2012) calls this commitment to re-membering an "act of decolonization" (p. 3). She entreats us to unlearn and learn anew so that we can "understand ways of being and knowing that have been marginalized in the world and formal education" (p. 4) and then use that knowledge to invest in transforming policy and practice.

How Did We Get Here?

It is not a news flash that European powers, in the interest of control and wealth, claimed lands around the world that were not theirs to claim. Flags were raised and pronouncements of "discovery" were made in lands that had been inhabited, self-governed, and cherished by Indigenous Peoples for centuries (Trouillot, 1995; Zinn, 2015).

For this oppressive plan to succeed, it was necessary for colonizers to propagandize their efforts by presenting concepts such as "The Age of Discovery" and "The Civilization of Man" (Kendi, 2016). To do so, they inaccurately portrayed Indigenous Peoples as less intelligent, uncivilized, and barbaric "with an elaborateness of detail of which no former world had ever dreamed" (Du Bois, 1920, p. 460). Through accounts that Maori researcher Linda Tuhiwai Smith (1999) calls "travelers' tales" (p. 2), colonizers framed themselves as "'heroes', 'discoverers', and 'adventurers'" (p. 21) while presenting Indigenous Peoples through "images of the cannibal chief, the red Indian, the witch doctor" (p. 8). Dominant cultural groups were taught to look "past people of Color as a wasteland of non-achievement" (p. 8). Christian missionaries furthered this narrative propagating descriptions of Indigenous Peoples as "higher order savages who deserved salvation" (p. 34). Official documents like the U.S. Declaration of Independence fortified these views by institutionalizing language like "merciless Indian savages."

The notion of race, also essential to the success of this scheme, was invented as a mechanism to justify dominance, enslavement, and genocide (Watkins, 2001) and a way to create division between working class Europeans—largely indentured servants and poor White farmers—and enslaved Africans and their descendants. This bolstered the notion of White supremacy as a useful tool for rationalizing control "even as [in the United States] whites endeavored to form a new nation built on the ideals of equality, liberty, and justice for all" (Alexander, 2012, p. 25).

The Role of Schools in Perpetuating Eurocentrism

In schools, curricula were designed to promote and sustain this ideology, teaching European-ness/Whiteness as superior (Roediger, 2007; Watkins, 2001). In fact, schooling was "the major agency for imposing this positional superiority over knowledge, language, and culture" (Smith, 1999, p. 67). Indigenous children were taught "new names for places that they and their parents had lived for generations" (pp. 53–54). Maps were created to reinforce the positioning of Indigenous lands "on the periphery of the world" (p. 38). Curricula were designed to "annihilate . . . [Indigenous] people's belief in their names, in their languages, in their environments, in their heritage of struggle, in their unity, in their capacities and ultimately in themselves" (Thiong'o, 2005, p. 2).

This led to incomplete and inaccurate learning in schools today as institutionally sanctioned accounts of history were passed from generation to generation.

Taught via the very systems that oppressed them, African descendants and Indigenous students were and continue to be alienated from their own "history, geography, music, and other aspects of culture" (Smith, 1999, p. 38), while European and European-descendant students and their histories continue to be centered and celebrated. Not only do our history books omit or barely mention African and other Indigenous contributors to the knowledge that guides our world today, but there is much we are not taught about why curriculum is so White-ified in the first place. As Carmen said:

> Even at my adult age until we were writing this book, I didn't know that the American government set up Indian Boarding Schools to take away traditions, beliefs, language, even the names of Native American children. I didn't know about sundown towns across America where African Americans, Mexican Americans, Native Americans, Jews, and Chinese Americans did the work in the town but had to leave by sundown.

This "epicenter of Whiteness rooted in colonization" (personal communication, Michael Dominguez, February 24, 2017) led to a kind of training of the mind, an "educat[ion] in whiteness" (Castagno, 2014, p. 4) through the effective silencing or distorting of much of the world's history. Although this can be a difficult reality for some people to confront, for educators it can be liberating. Once we realize how we got to this point, we can move toward creating a new status quo by dedicating ourselves to relearning and reteaching histories and using knowledge to impact policy and practice (Battiste, 2013).

So, What Do We Do?

In 2014, Molefi Kete Asante wrote that "our educational systems do not need tune-ups; they need an overhaul of their educational engines" (p. 51). Let's consider what educators can do as we commit to this kind of change.

Acknowledge the need for change. First, we need to acknowledge that schooling still suffers fallout from the "colonial bomb" (Thiong'o, 2005, p. 2) that attempted to wipe out, misrepresent, and marginalize African and other Indigenous cultures (Castagno, 2014; Roediger, 2007). In fact, the U.S. Declaration of Independence did not mean independence for Indigenous and enslaved peoples from their oppressors, but merely independence for colonizers from their European homelands (Waziyatawin & Yellow Bird, 2005). Examples of ongoing colonization are evident everywhere in schools and society once we develop the eye to notice it.

A clear illustration of present-day colonial mentality can be found in reactions to the 2017 premiere of the film *Hidden Figures* (Gigliotti & Melfi, 2016). The movie retells events in the history of the U.S. space program, illuminating the fundamental roles of African American mathematicians Katherine Johnson, Dorothy Vaughan, and Mary Jackson. Their analytic genius was instrumental in making the first human space travel possible. Viewing the film, people across the country began to ask, "Why didn't we know about them before?" and "If I didn't know this, what else is missing from my education?" Though this suppression of history is revealing enough, a closer look provides an example of colonizing actions in the form of completely inaccurate retellings. The film highlighted a White male lead taking antiracist action by dramatically pulling down the "Colored" sign posted above a bathroom door. In actuality, the incident never occurred. The director's explanation revealed the same kind of whitewashing of reality that occurred centuries ago. He explained that the incident was fabricated because the film "needed White people who do the right thing" (Willis, 2017). Although artistic license occurs regularly in films, this is an important example of how easily the colonization of our minds can take hold (Thiong'o, 2005).

Again, the voices of family members of children in Carmen and Janice's classrooms bring clarity as, over and over, they described the colonial legacy of Whiteness evident in their own schooling and the need for change in their children's formal education. Ms. Sims, for example, was emphatic when talking about her own Eurocratic schooling in contrast to what she wants for her own children:

> [My schooling] was all about George Washington, Benjamin Franklin, all the White people. Not saying that's bad because part of our history is White people, too. But the only time we saw or heard anything about Black people was during Black History month. As soon as March 1 came, you better believe they didn't speak about it. It just wasn't taught. But as you become a parent, you say, "Wait a minute, that's not right." I want kids to know that Black people are great people that have done great things also. I want them to know that we played a key role building this society.

Commit to relearning. Movements in Canada (Battiste, 2013), New Zealand (Skerrett, 2014), and the United States (Patel, 2016) answer the call to overhaul pedagogy by working to decolonize curriculum. They commit to listening to and learning from African and other Indigenous Peoples who rewrite and re-right (Smith, 1999) histories of accomplishment, oppression, and resistance. So, next steps are to take up the challenge to "critically learn" (Dominguez, 2017, p. 234), recognizing that when we do not challenge colonized accounts as "the centre of legitimate knowledge" (Smith, 1999, p. 66), we teach antithetically to the purposes of culturally relevant pedagogy. Once we commit to relearning, the floodgates open and we are drawn to questioning historical accounts and seeking Indigenous points of view in any way we can. As Janice reminds us, if we put our students first, the decision to invest in relearning is not difficult to make:

> When I think about how my social studies books had only one paragraph or page about Martin Luther King, Jr., or Rosa Parks, and how my history came to me outside of school, I know that I can't risk my students missing out on that or other information missing from the history books. So, I have to be sure I take advantage of the access I have to knowledge and go after it.

RESOURCES FOR RE-MEMBERING HISTORIES

Au, W., Brown, A. L, & and Calderón, D. (2016). *Reclaiming the Multicultural Roots of U.S. Curriculum*
Battiste, M. (2013). *Reclaiming Indigenous Voice and Vision*
Dunbar-Ortiz, R. (2014). *An Indigenous People's History of the United States*
Kendi, I. X. (2016). *Stamped from the Beginning*
Loewen, J. (2007). *Lies My Teachers Told Me*
Rodney, W. (2011). *How Europe Underdeveloped Africa*
Thiong'o, N. (2005). *Decolonizing the Mind*
Trouillot, M. (1995). *Silencing the Past*
Zinn, H. (2015). *A People's History of the United States*

QUESTIONS TO GUIDE RE-MEMBERING

- What is my plan for seeking untold or mistold histories and hidden figures?
- How will I engage my students in researching to re-member with me?
- How will I plan for teaching that centers and normalizes hidden figures and histories?
- How will my teaching engage students in learning to question historical representations of Peoples and seek Indigenous accounts?

Committing to relearning through a critical lens, we can begin to move toward teaching that is fuller and more equitable. We can be energized knowing that this work is not "*against* history; it is *for* history, correct, accurate history" (Asante, 2017, p. 67); it is "not anti-White; it is pro-human" (p. 82).

"AMERICA OWES ITSELF"

Culturally relevant teaching requires adopting a critical habit of mind so we can work against ideology "that justifies inequity" (King & Akua, 2012, p. 724). We can begin that journey by embracing the kind of good love that requires identifying and addressing self- and institutional biases; taking our lead from trusting, respectful relationships with families; relearning histories; and committing to change. We are inspired by educators who do so with courage, conviction, and joy, recognizing that "holding tightly to what is presently known" (Patel, 2016, p. 95) keeps us from confronting the injustices of the past and present. It is not just a debt we owe to ourselves and our students, it is what America owes itself (Coates, 2017).

CHAPTER 3

Starting the Year in Culturally Relevant Ways

Your classroom had an environment of Black history. You could feel the vibe when you walked in the door. You had it on the walls, in the halls, on the doors, always talking about it. You could actually read the walls and find out more about Black history all year, not just a particular month or day or whatever. —Ms. Frazier, mother of Tahiem (1st grader)

Walking into Janice and Carmen's classroom at the beginning of the year, you will see a Sierra Leone heritage corner filled with artifacts to help children learn about connections between West Africa and the United States (Chapter 6), baskets loaded with books by and about African Americans, and posters and photographs of famous African Americans filling the walls. This echoes the call by Asante (2017) for *every classroom* to be filled with reflections of African, African American, and Indigenous genius: "astrophysicists and astronauts, the poets and novelists, the award-winning dramatists, dancers, and choreographers, the philosophers and educational innovators . . . a veritable festival of talent should stare down at students at every turn" (p. 24).

Well aware of the White dominance that their students will experience through much of their schooling, Janice and Carmen know that if they do not center African and African American contributions and histories, it is likely that their students will not experience it anywhere else. Janice and Carmen do this no matter the demographic of their classrooms. Though they do not neglect Native American, Latinx, Asian, and European American histories, authors, artists, and scientists, they know that the tide must be turned so that all students come to know the brilliance of Africa and African America. Thus, the choices they make about preparing classrooms for the first day of school matter. In this chapter, we share ways that Carmen and Janice started the school year by re-centering African and African American heritage as important for every child while setting the tone for developing critical consciousness as way of life in their classroom.

SETTING UP THE CLASSROOM

Each summer, standing in Janice and Carmen's classrooms with boxes of books, shelves covered to protect them from summer dust, and furniture in disarray, we considered the children who would soon walk through the doors. We were there to set up the classroom but also to prepare for a transformation of the mind. Family members let us know that this is essential because, in their short lives, their children have already been exposed to what one mother called "a barrage of Whiteness"— school spaces where there is little or no evidence that people of color contribute significantly to the world. Other family members talked about the avoidance of race in classrooms dominated by "themes like polka dots or animals," describing the non-human themes as a default to Whiteness. This parallels studies of young Black and White children who, when asked about the race of cartoon animals or yellow LEGO dolls, assigned Whiteness because it was so normalized as dominant in their worlds (Husband, 2016; Miller, 2015). In contrast, in Janice and Carmen's classrooms, Blackness was as richly represented as Whiteness—intentionally foregrounded in books, materials, and instructional content.

Setting the Tone: Social Justice Happens Here

Carmen and Janice want students to recognize their potential as social justice players from the beginning of the year. Carmen often initiates this with the design of her classroom door and engagements that follow. One year, wanting to greet her students with the message that we are all inheritors of a great legacy in the fight against injustice, she decorated the door with a large sign that read, "Mrs. Tisdale's Class, Keepers of the Dream." On the door, she posted photographs of civil rights leader Dr. Martin Luther King, Jr., surrounded by the children's names.

After the children entered the classroom, put away their belongings, and found their seats, Carmen drew their attention to the door: "Did you notice what was on the door when you came in this morning? What did you see?" Carmen asked what the students knew about Dr. King. Many of them had heard his name but knew little else. The first days of school were full of discussion as Carmen read aloud each day from a collection of picture books about Dr. King. She introduced his *I Have a Dream* speech and asked questions like: "Why did Dr. King have a dream?" "What was happening in the country that made his dream necessary?" "Do we still need his dream today?" "Why?" "What can we do about it?" Carmen explained her motive and purpose:

> First, they have to understand the dream and why the dream was and still is necessary. They may have heard of Dr. King, but do children realize the big job they have as keepers of his dream?

Carmen decided to introduce Dr. King on the first day of school when she realized that she had merely been scratching the surface of what the students needed to know:

PICTURE BOOKS ABOUT DR. MARTIN LUTHER KING, JR.

Evans, S. E. (2016). *We March*
Farris, C. K. (2006). *My Brother Martin*
Farris, C. K. (2008). *March On! The Day My Brother Martin Changed the World*
King, M. L. & Nelson, K. (2012). *I Have a Dream*
Michelson, R. (2013). *As Good as Anybody: Martin Luther King, Jr., and Abraham Joshua Heschel's Amazing March Toward Freedom*
Rappaport, D. (2007). *Martin's Big Words*
Ringgold, F. (1998). *My Dream of Martin Luther King*
Watkins, A. F. (2010). *My Uncle Martin's Big Heart*

When I first began teaching about Dr. King, it was only during Black history month. My students seemed to walk away retaining only two facts: He was killed and he had a dream, which some of them took literally. They needed to get beyond typical stories about his life and death to think about the difference his work made and the role they could play in the work yet to be done. I had been underestimating my students.

To move away from an overly-simplified introduction of Dr. King, from the first days of the year, Carmen began building the idea of the class as a Dream Team—people who can make a difference. She explained that this was a job that was not to be taken lightly. Carmen took a photograph of the 2nd-grade Dream Team grouped around Dr. King's photos on the classroom door. The children wrote about their dreams, starting with goals for themselves and plans for meeting those goals. At the beginning of the year, their goals were largely academic and behavioral: to be a better reader, to finish my work, to be kind to my friends. As the year went on, the goals focused beyond the classroom to larger issues of justice (Chapter 7), all emanating from Carmen's establishment of social justice talk as a part of daily discourse from the first day of school.

Alphabet Wall: Community Touchstones

In addition to establishing students' roles as justice players, we work to help students recognize their abilities as readers and writers from the first days of school. We want students to know that their homes and communities are full of literacies and that there is much they can already read. One way we do this is via the classroom alphabet chart. We post 11-by-14-inch letters of the alphabet across the top 2 feet of one wall and onto the adjacent wall. On the first day of school, we take photos of each child, and print them as 8-by-10-inch copies. The second morning, we work one to one with the children to mount the photos on brightly colored construction paper and label them with the children's names in letters large enough to be seen across the room. On subsequent days, as the children gather on the carpet, Carmen and Janice hold up the photos one at a time and ask the children to find "their letter" on the alphabet chart: Tt for Traion, Ss for Simone, and so on. Guided by the children, they post each photo under the appropriate letter, talking about their names and other words that start like or have patterns like those in their names.

Carmen and Janice also bring in photos of landmarks in the children's communities: the Family Dollar store sign, the McDonald's logo, Anthony's Dairy Bar (a neighborhood favorite), Kentucky Fried Chicken. They guide the children in making community connections and learning about letter–sound relationships as they decide where the photos should be posted on the alphabet chart (Figure 3.1):

> What is this photo? Bojangles! Who eats at Bojangles? Let's look at that word and say it together. Listen to the sound you hear at the beginning of *Bojangles*. Do we know anyone in our classroom whose name starts like Bojangles? Brianna! Look at our alphabet chart and find Brianna's picture. What letter is above it? That's the letter B. Where should we put the photo of Bojangles on the wall? Under the B, like Brianna. What other words do you know that start with B?

This first-week exercise creates a resource grounded in the children's worlds and used throughout the year. Janice and Carmen teach their students how to make analogies between words on the alphabet chart and new words that they want to use as writers and readers. Janice explains to them:

> When you are writing a story or a letter to a friend and you need to spell a word, say the word to yourself and think, "Do I know another word that starts like this word (or ends like it or has a chunk in it like this word)?" I want to write the word *baseball*. I say it to myself and think about the first sound I hear. Do I know a friend's name or a place in my community that starts with that sound? Where can I look to find the letter I need?

The alphabet wall sends a clear message that learning to read begins *with* the students' worlds not outside their worlds. It locates them within the literacies of their communities *and* the literacies of schooling, letting students know that they are already skillful and literate while supporting further learning. Years after she was in Carmen's class, Sameka captured the power of this syncretic act—blending home and school knowledge—as she explained:

> You had *our* places—churches, stores, on the wall. I never saw no other teacher who had pictures like that. I loved using those pictures to help with my spelling and reading.

Most powerful, however, is the way the larger-than-life photos of the students and community places shout relevance to anyone who walks in the door. At the

Figure 3.1. Alphabet Wall with Student and Community Touchstones

end of the school year, the photos are given to the students as a keepsake. Carmen and Janice love reflecting on the pictures as they hand them out and talk about how the students have grown.

Book Collections

Building and organizing the classroom book collection is another foundational task for every teacher at the beginning of the year. For the culturally relevant classroom, this takes careful thought. Although strides have been made in the past couple of decades to diversify children's books, the reality is that we have a long way to go. In 2016, only 90 of the 3,200 books published that year and reviewed by the Cooperative Children's Book Center (2017) were written by or about African Americans. Twenty-two books were written by and about Native Americans, 101 by and about Latinx people, and 212 by or about Asian Americans.

Instructional texts are even worse. The overwhelming majority of books developed for small- and large-group instruction reflect what Gangi (2008) called the "unbearable Whiteness of literacy instruction." They are dominated by White characters or animals and when persons of color are included, they are often depicted in stereotypical, one-dimensional ways. As Janice said, "You see stories that use names like Mrs. Ramos or José or Javon or Kadiesha, but the stories have little to do with who they are. They just put those names in there to give the illusion of diversity."

Examining book collections. Carmen and Susi felt the Whiteness of instructional book collections firsthand when, one Friday evening, they spent a couple of hours looking through the school's bookroom for books to send home for reading practice. Although the school's demographic was 99% African American students,

---

RESOURCES FOR JUDGING THE AUTHENTICITY OF DIVERSITY IN CHILDREN'S BOOKS

- Reading Diversity Lite (Teacher's Edition): A Tool for Selecting Diverse Texts: www.tolerance.org/sites/default/files/general/Reading%20 Diversity%20Lite—Teacher%27s%20Edition2.pdf
- Social Justice Books Guide for Selecting Anti-Bias Children's Books: socialjusticebooks.org/guide-for-selecting-anti-bias-childrens-books/
- Ten Quick Ways to Analyze Children's Books for Racism and Sexism: readingspark.wordpress.com/adoption-childrens-literature/ten-quick-ways-to-analyze-childrens-books-for-racism-and-sexism/

---

out of hundreds of instructional texts, only a handful depicted African Americans, and those that did were stereotyped or unrelated to the students' worlds. In addition, there were no books to serve as windows for the students into other worlds, and no books depicting Latinx or Native American families, no bilingual texts, no books with gay, lesbian, or transgender family members; none with families cared for by grandmothers, uncles, or fictive kin; no books with Muslim, Jewish, or Hindu families. It was effectively an "erasure" (Butler, 2017, p. 153) of all but White, mother-father, middle-class, English-only families. The Whiteness of the book room sent strong messages about who mattered and who did not, messages that were not lost on the students. Second-grader Brion told Carmen, "When there are only books about White people, it makes everyone feel like only White people can do stuff."

No excuse. The low percentage of trade books and instructional texts by and about persons of color is not only frustrating, but is a form of institutional bias on the part of publishing companies and educational selection committees. However, it is *not* an excuse for failing to fill classrooms with books that richly reflect our diverse society. We can find them using any number of antibias book recommendation and evaluation websites.

Janice and Carmen work with the school media specialist to order a wide range of books by and about people of color. They are careful not to give the "illusion of inclusion" (King & Swartz, 2014, p. 7) by ordering only a few token volumes. Instead, they order a *preponderance of books* by and about persons of color. Prior to ordering, they meticulously examine book reviews to guard against stereotype and misrepresentation and to find books that will engage their particular groups of students.

Another way we address the lack of representation in the instructional book collection is by creating books with and for the students (see examples throughout this book). We develop what Alfred Tatum (2009) called enabling texts to join students' "in-school and out-of-school lives" (p. 1). Our intent is to affirm students and their communities while broadening their views of the world and building literacy proficiency.

RESOURCES FOR FINDING DIVERSITY-CENTERED CHILDREN'S BOOKS

- Cooperative Children's Book Center, College of Education, University of Wisconsin: ccbc.education.wisc.edu
- Social Justice Books/Teaching for Change: socialjusticebooks.org/booklists/
- Teaching for Change: www.teachingforchange.org/selecting-anti-bias-books
- The Brown Bookshelf: thebrownbookshelf.com
- We Need Diverse Books: medium.com/embrace-race/childrens-books-featuring-kids-of-color-being-themselves-because-that-s-enough-36aa15c94d44

THE FIRST WEEKS OF SCHOOL

This is the day I meet the children I will be with for the next 180 days. I don't take the day lightly. I want to establish a sense of family in my classroom. I tell them how much I love them and that I'm their mom at school. I offer assurance that I will look after them while they are with me. —Carmen

Like the classroom setup, the decisions we make and engagements we plan during the first weeks of school set the tone for the coming year. Described in this section, Janice and Carmen establish welcoming, affirming, culturally relevant classrooms in a variety of ways.

Creating Homes Away from Home

Janice and Carmen see themselves as their students' mothers at school. They work to establish that relationship from the first days of the year with the goal of creating classrooms as homes away from home. "It's simple," Janice says. "You take care of students like they are your own." The children's comments often reflected this sense of othermothering (Foster, 1997; Williams, 2011), as did kindergartner Keith's words when he sought reassurance from Carmen one morning: "Ms. Tisdale," he said, "you're our mama at school, right?" "Yes, I sure am," Carmen replied. "I'm your mom at school. It's my job to love and take care of you while you're with me at school." Janice's story about Ms. King and Katia illustrates the importance of establishing this home-away-from-home feeling in the eyes of family members as well as in the eyes of the children.

Every morning during the first week of school, after taking Katia into the kindergarten classroom, Ms. King stood at the classroom door looking in. Every morning, Janice asked Ms. King if she wanted to join the class. "No, I'm just watching," Ms. King would say, sometimes standing there for an hour or more. One day, she accepted Janice's offer and came in to sit at the side of the room. When the children went to recess, Janice asked if she would like to help prepare take-home folders. While they worked, they talked. Ms. King explained that Katia had been so tiny at birth that she always worried something would happen to her. Janice reassured Ms. King that Katia was in good hands. However, more important than verbal reassurance was Janice's demonstration of respect for Ms. King's need to stay until she felt comfortable enough to leave. The next day, Ms. King walked Katia to the classroom door and left with the other mothers and grandmothers. She had witnessed Janice's othermothering for herself. She felt confident that Janice would care for her child.

Heartstrings and High Expectations

Janice and Carmen found that establishing the classroom as a home away from home was essential to being able to hold students to high expectations. This is what researcher Judith Kleinfeld (1975) called "warm demanding" teaching—exuding personal warmth as foundational to "actively demanding high quality academic work" (p. 26). Not surprisingly, Kleinfeld found that students worked harder and achieved at higher levels in classrooms when teachers *first* developed genuinely caring relationships and *then* insisted on excellence.

Geneva Gay (2010) connected Kleinfeld's work to culturally relevant teaching when she wrote about culturally relevant caring as that which joins warmth with "settl[ing] for nothing less than high achievement" (p. 49). Janice talks about this as "finding the heartstring," the loving connection that will allow her to establish high expectations. Ms. Myers, a community elder who worked at the school and spent much time observing Janice's relationships with students, captured that characteristic:

> Ms. Baines, you love your kids and I've seen that. You have playtime but
> when it's time to be serious, you close that door, you say, "Let's be quiet, time
> to get to the books. Let's learn." Your students know you love them, that you
> believe in them, and that you really want them to learn.

Teaching in this way builds on a legacy from African American schools prior to desegregation where students were "nourished, supported, protected, encouraged [but also] held accountable on personal, academic, and civic levels" (Gay, 2010, p. 53). Adults from those generations remember teachers' "faith and conviction in [their] abilities . . . insisting that [they] have high aspirations to be the best that they could be" (Siddle Walker, 1996, p. 53). Mr. Ford, a school board member and one of the students' oral history interviewees (Chapter 5), explained the sanctuary and lift that schools provided for him as a child:

> [We were taught] that no one could make you feel bad without your
> permission. We were instilled with, "Hey, you're brilliant, you're talented,
> you're gifted and we're not going to allow you to fail." They instilled a sense
> of worth and value and uplift that was second to none.

Much of this kind of support was lost during desegregation, when White teachers replaced Black teachers or students were bused to all-White schools (Siddle Walker, 1996). Even the most loving White teachers were often guided by negative stereotypes and/or White savior attitudes—"the poor Black kids from the inner city"—with no firsthand knowledge of the strength, expertise, and history of Black communities. Expectations were often lowered as teachers taught down to ill-informed assumptions (Gershenson et al., 2016). As James Baldwin (1962) wrote, "You were not expected to aspire to excellence. You were expected to make peace with mediocrity" (p. 7).

Geneva Gay (2010) calls this culture of low expectation "academic neglect" (p. 55). Ladson-Billings (2003) writes about it as giving students "permission to fail" (p. 110). With this in mind, Janice and Carmen's primary objective during the first days of school is to establish loving connections, letting students know that their teachers see and believe in their brilliance so that students will want to live up to their high expectations and mediocrity will not be a choice. Years later, Javon's mother, Ms. Williams, recalled how important this was to her son's success in Janice's 1st grade. She told Janice: "You knew Javon could do it. He would act up sometimes but from the first day to the last, you loved my son enough to never give up."

Passing Love and Caring for the Community

As a part of developing her classroom as a home away from home, Carmen engages students in a tradition that she calls "Passing the Love." She uses it to initiate a communal, caring tone in her classroom. On the first day of school, the children sit in a circle on the carpet and pass a stuffed heart mascot named Love. Holding Love signifies when it is students' turn to share their names and something that they love or want their classmates to know about them. Carmen starts with a demonstration: "My name is Ms. Tisdale. I love to dance." Soon, patterns emerge about individual interests and commonalities: riding bikes, having a pet, pink as a favorite color, having brothers and sisters.

Carmen builds from these connections to talk about classroom community. She draws on the African ethic that caring for the community "is to care for the self, and to care for the self is to care for the group" (Siddle Walker & Snarey, 2004, p. 136). Everyone in Carmen's class has a job to do from the first day: answering the classroom phone, passing out and picking up papers, taking care of recycling, watering the plants, sharpening pencils, logging on to the computers each morning and turning them off in the afternoon. Carmen tells the students that they are their brothers' and sisters' keepers: Neglecting your job lets down the whole community. Carmen also emphasizes that every member of the class is responsible for supporting every other student's brilliance. This includes supporting each other's opportunity to grow. She tells them: "Don't blurt out the answer. When you do, you don't help build each other's brains. Let everyone else have time to think."

We Are Family

From day one, Janice lets the children know that they are a part of a classroom family. One year, she reinforced this by engaging the children in creating a book inspired by the Sister Sledge song "We Are Family" (Edwards & Rodgers, 1979). The children wrote about things they liked to do. Each page followed a simple, predictable pattern: "My name is India. I like to ride my bike." Janice created the pages as PowerPoint slides with the children's photos and illustrations imported into them. In this way, the book could be projected onto the Smartboard for whole-group reading and also printed and bound as books used for small-group work. Multiple copies were placed in book baskets for independent reading.

The book they created, We Are Family, helped build a sense of belonging *and* served as a text for the first literacy lessons of the year. The students were excited to read something about *them*. The book's predictable structure and familiar content meant that they could read it and see themselves as readers from the first day of school. We Are Family was the first of what would become a rich collection of class-made books that formed an essential part of Janice's classroom library.

All About Miss Baines and All About Me

Along with We Are Family, one year, Janice made a book to introduce herself to the students. She styled the book after a stepping pattern she observed the children performing when she spent time in their neighborhood. She noticed them chanting words to a particular rhythm:

> I got this boy on my mind.
> All of the time.
> I have his picture in my book.
> Don't you worry about his look.

Janice also knew that stepping was a direct descendant of African American dance forms from the late 1800s and, before that, from Africa and the African Diaspora. So, drawing on African legacy and students' community knowledge, Janice created the book All About Miss Baines, written to the cadence of the stepping rhythm:

> Miss Baines is my name
> Teaching is my game.
> I have books on my mind
> All of the time.
> I have a big family.
> They make me happy!
> Pink is my color.
> You will love knowing Miss Baines.

On the first day of school, as Janice read aloud, "I have books on my mind, all of the time," the children immediately connected to the rhythm they knew. Janice continued, projecting the book's pages on the Smartboard:

Janice: [Pointing to the photo of her family reunion and reading] I have a big family.

Children: Ohhh! That's your family?

Janice: That's *some* of my family. I have a lot more. That's my grandfather, that's my sister, that's my little cousin and that's me. [Then pointing to the words again] And then it says, "They make me, what?"

Children: Happy!

After the children read and enjoyed the book many times, Janice helped them merge home literacies with conventions of schooling as she used *All About Miss Baines* to point out text features such as the title page and literacy skills like left-to-right directionality, word patterns, and punctuation. On the last pages, she listed the high-frequency words found in the book (Figure 3.2) and explained to the children: "You see these words all the time. You can read them in *All About Miss Baines* so you can read them in every other book you see!" Again, the syncretic power was clear: "They were excited because they didn't know that we could put something they need to learn in school into something they already know."

All About Miss Baines led to the children's *All About Me* books. Following the same format and stepping rhythm, the children created books about themselves. As the first student-authored books of the year, the predictable format allowed the children to feel immediate success not only as readers but as writers (Figure 3.3).

When I Was a Little Girl

Carmen also created a book to introduce herself during the first week of school. Hers was titled, *When I Was a Little Girl*. Glimpsing into Carmen's life through the book, the students learned about her home as the "go-to house" where her mother gave everyone popsicles, her love of swimming and being on the school's swim team, tractor-tire rolls, running in nearby fields, and walking a long way to find the best plums. The book also helped Carmen and the students connect with each other. For example, Isaiah, the football player in the class, shared that he tackled a big guy on the field just as Carmen did when she was a little girl. He loved when Carmen read aloud, "Nobody could believe that I had no fear to tackle him!"

Carmen initially thought of the book as a creative way to allow the children into her world, but the experience far exceeded her expectations. Predictable text was printed in blue at the top of each page echoing the book's title: *When I was a little girl . . .* followed on each page by a different story from their lives (Figure

Figure 3.2. Cover and Closing Pages from *All About Ms. Baines*

ALL ABOUT MISS BAINES

By, Miss Janice Baines and
Her First Grade Class

Can you read these High Frequency Words
from *All About Miss Baines?*
Can you find them in this book?

about	love	will
all	make	time
big	me	
Happy	my	
have	name	
I	of	
is	on	

If you can read this book,
you can read these words too!

Miss Baines is my **name**.
Teaching is my **game**.

name
game
same
tame
frame
flame
came
shame

Word Study: word chunks
and word families.

If you can read this book,
you can read these words too!

 Pink is my color.

pink
think
stink
link
mink
rink
sink
wink

Word Study: word chunks
and word families.

Figure 3.3. Pages from Students' *All About Me* Books Following the Format of *All About Miss Baines*

3.4). This meant that beginning readers could read something on every page—the predictable text—while broadening their reading abilities by transacting with the more complex narrative that told the stories.

First-grader Marcus was particularly drawn to Carmen's book. At age 6, Marcus had already internalized the belief that he was not intelligent. His brothers and sister called him dumb. He rarely raised his hand during lessons and typically refused to read. However, *When I Was a Little Girl* struck a chord for him. Marcus harbored a copy of the book in his desk for weeks, reading it over and over. It held all of the characteristics of a supportive text for an emergent or reluctant reader: It was a book that he wanted to read, it reflected elements of his world, he could read something on every page immediately, and there was just enough challenging text to move him toward next steps as a reader.

Carmen's book also helped establish the classroom as a space for critically conscious conversations. This foundation was laid when she read aloud about a racist incident that occurred in her childhood. The page read:

> I remember being in the shower one day after swim practice. I heard one of my White teammates inviting all of the White members of the swim team to her house for a birthday sleepover that night. I got all excited at the idea of going. But when I got out of the shower, she didn't invite me. I was very sad.

The story provided an opening for talk about why Carmen, as one of the few African Americans on her school's swim team, was not invited to the party, how it made her feel, and what the students might do if something similar happened to them or if they witnessed it happening to other children. It let students know from the beginning of the year that it was important to talk about race and racism in this classroom.

Years later, children fondly remembered *When I Was a Little Girl*. Sameka, by then in 6th grade, recalled, "Regular teachers just tell you their name, [but] you introduced yourself with a book about your family and when you were a little girl!" Ms. Sims, Sameka's mother, commented on the way the book created a model for students to feel comfortable enough to share their own stories:

> [Sameka] was so excited. She brought [the book] home for us to read it with her. A lot of times, you ask people to talk about themselves and they shut down. I think by seeing you do yours, it made it cool [so she thought], "You know, I'm going to tell about my family, too."

"I Am Brilliant!"

Concern for children like Marcus, the child who believed the negative profiles imposed on him, is why Carmen begins each year letting students know that they are capable, strong, and brilliant. This is a part of Carmen's commitment to acting on her own critical consciousness. She explained:

Figure 3.4. Pages from *When I Was a Little Girl*

This is me!

Carmen Michelle Tisdale.

At school, I'm called,
Mrs. Tisdale.

At home, I'm called
Michelle or just Chelle.

And some people call me
Carmen.

When I was a
little girl, I was
on the swim
team. I was
really good.
I loved being on
the swim team.

It is troubling that young children so early in life have come to believe they are not intelligent, particularly Black students because they receive that message so many places. So, I take on the charge to help them know and believe they are brilliant and capable of great academic success.

On the first day of school, Carmen introduces the phrase "I am brilliant!" by asking the students what the word *brilliant* means. She listens and then shares what it means to her: "It is the brightness of a light. You're all brilliant because your smarts shine. I look at you and see your intelligence glowing." This becomes a mantra used throughout the year as Carmen stops to remind them, "You were so great at this because you're what?" The students shout in response, "Brilliant!"

The call-and-response nature of these proclamations echo traditions of African teaching and storytelling. Teachers can talk about and point out these connections by using video clips and picture books to share ways that this discourse style influenced gospel, blues, jazz, the question-and-answer style of chants during the civil rights movement, church, and hip-hop (Kebede, 2017; Smitherman, 1977).

Just as with high expectations, however, these declarations do little good without, as Michele Foster (1997) wrote, "tak[ing] responsibility for finding meaningful, motivating methods that work" (p. 32). Simply telling "students they are smart and . . . repeatedly teaching content that is not intellectually challenging affirms that, in reality, the students are not seen as smart or intellectually capable" (Perry, Steele, & Hilliard, 2004, p. 103). The practices in this book represent our convictions about taking responsibility for meaningful methods, while proclamations of brilliance were important class touchstones of affirmation all year long.

I'm a Boundless Scholar

During the first weeks of school, Janice also introduces a daily ritual through which students declare their brilliance: "I am somebody. I am capable. I am loveable. I am beautiful. I am a scholar." Janice teaches definitions for the word *scholar* and, as the weeks go by, the students define it for themselves: "A scholar is smart," "Scholars are people who can learn stuff," "Scholars got big brains, like *I'm* a scholar." In this way, Janice creates opportunities for students to self-identify as scholars *and* learn new vocabulary.

Janice connects these declarations to deeper learning. She reads the picture book *Boundless Grace* (Hoffman, 1995) and the children investigate the word *boundless*. One, year, checking a virtual dictionary, they found the definition: "infinite or vast; unlimited." Janice told them: "That's just like you all. You are brilliant and *boundless* scholars. That means there are no limits to what you can learn. Your learning is *infinite*. It goes on forever and ever."

Janice told the children that boundless scholars question the world around them. She explained that scholars give their opinions and support them. She celebrated their thinking with further affirmations: "You're thinking like a scholar!" and "I never thought about it that way. Your *scholarly* mind helped me think in a new way."

Soon after this conversation, Janice and her students created a song to celebrate this scholarly spirit. Using the rhythms of a chant Janice remembered from her own childhood, a portion of the song went like this:

> I love being a scholar! Boom!
> I love the way they treat me! Boom!
> I love the way they teach me! Boom!
> I'm a Boundless Scholar! Boom!
> I can read around the room and learn for knowledge.
> Can't stop now, we're on our way to college.
> Millions of books on my mind, sounds and letters are fun.
> Where I'm from, we get it done.

Figure 3.5. Pages from *I'm a Boundless Scholar*

The children illustrated the lyrics and Janice made them into a book. *I'm a Boundless Scholar* was added to the morning ritual and the classroom library (Figure 3.5). The lyrics became a part of the classroom lexicon: "Boom!" Janice would say, "That math equation you just figured out! *You* are a scholar." "Wow! You just read that page all by yourself? You are a *boundless* scholar!" These in-the-moment connections to a beloved chant were often just the trigger the students needed to redirect and refocus.

Soon, the children were using words from *Boundless Scholar* in their writing, learning that they could use familiar resources to create their own texts: "I know where that word is in *Boundless Scholar*, Ms. Baines." Often, children would pick up a trade book and find a word that they knew from *Boundless Scholar*. Janice explained, "They may have to sing the song in their minds in order to get to that word, but they can do it."

Name Stories

Another beginning-of-the-year engagement is one that Susi uses with preservice teachers as they work with children in schools. Concerned when children's names are degraded as they are mispronounced or changed to suit the comfort level of teachers, Susi explains to student teachers that the denigration of students' names constitutes a linguicist microaggression, a result of Eurocentric bias (Kohli & Solórzano, 2012). After seeking students' name stories from family members, the university students and children create pieces of writing telling the stories of each child's name—why their families chose their names and/or why they love their children's names. The children and their university partners use their writing and a photo to create a page for a class name storybook that not only affirms pride in their own names, but allows them to hear and learn to appreciate the beauty and history in the names of their peers. One year, the students and children developed predictable text to introduce each name story and lead to the next story:

Tanisha is my name.
No Tanisha is the same.
Read along to find out.
What my name is all about.
[Here the child's name story is inserted.]
My name story has come to an end.
Turn the page and meet my friend.

Carmen reinvented the idea for her students by first creating a book telling her name story. Illustrated with photos of her parents and family, the book tells the story of how Carmen was named and why her name is important to her. Carmen reads the book aloud and then guides the children to interview their families to learn about their naming stories and about the day they came into their families' lives.

These ideas have also been beautifully enhanced by teachers like Alicia Boardman, who tells her students, "You should never let someone say your name wrong!" (Nash, Panther, & Arce-Boardman, 2017, p. 2), and then reads a range of picture books about the beauty of names and engages students in interviewing their families and writing their own name stories. Jessica Martell (Souto-Manning & Martell, 2016) and Carmen Llerena (Souto-Manning, Llerena, Martell, Salas, & Arce-Boardman, 2018) involve their students in researching their names, thereby building research and literacy skills as they honor one another's families, communities, and heritage.

Writing Topics and Learning About Imagery

Carmen and Janice want students to start the year feeling the power of their abilities as writers as well as readers. They focus in culturally relevant ways by teaching children that authors write about events, memories, and feelings that are meaningful—relevant—to them. Reading pictures books and pointing out how authors draw on their own lives to tell vivid stories provides a powerful introduction to this notion. Reading Rockets (www.readingrockets.org/books/interviews/) provides wonderful video clips of authors sharing their processes for children's viewing. Some of our favorites are Kwame Alexander, Alma Flor Ada, Brian Collier, Rita Williams-Garcia, E. B. Lewis, Patricia McKissack, Kadir Nelson, and Walter Dean Myers.

One year, Susi initiated a writerly focus on personal connections by reading Eloise Greenfield's (1986) poem "Honey, I Love" to Carmen's 2nd-graders. Susi stopped reading after each verse of the poem and asked the students to talk with a friend about experiences they were reminded of. They jotted down those memories as potential writing topics on a special page in their writing folders (Figure 3.6). This created a menu from which the children drafted writing pieces during the first months of school. For example, Marc listed topics such as "When I went to Charleston to see my brother," "When somebody pushed me," "When my mommy had a baby," and "When my hand got stuck in the car"—a treasure trove of writing topics to give purpose to writing throughout the year.

To guide students developing a first draft from one of the topics, Susi and Carmen used a variation of Georgia Heard's (1998) six-image strategy. They asked students to visualize their writing topic or memory—to put themselves in the moment of that memory—and then to jot down images by thinking about what they saw, heard, felt, wondered, and the quality of light in the memory (bright sun, overcast and rainy, dim lamp on the table, and so on). Carmen and Susi expanded this by guiding the students to look for details in their memories:

- What do you see in front of you? Behind you? Beneath you? Above you? Coming toward you? Walking away from you?
- What do you hear people saying? How are they saying it? Do you hear rain or wind? Do you hear silence? What breaks the silence? Do you hear crying or laughing? What does it sound like? Do you hear cars or trains or other sounds? Listen again. Listen more. Are the sounds loud or soft or screechy or calming or . . . ?

The combination of the writing topics list and the imagery exercise (Figure 3.6) established culturally relevant writing from the first weeks of school as students learned that writers find topics and vivid details by drawing from their own experiences.

Community Map

During the first weeks of school, Carmen continues to build on students' community knowledge by engaging them in creating a map of their community. Although mapping is not an uncommon activity in early childhood classrooms, Carmen uses it to build a further sense of communal belonging and show students what they know while addressing social studies and literacy standards.

The students use the same community landmarks posted on the alphabet wall (Bojangles, Anthony's Dairy Bar, Food Lion, and so forth) to create a large map on a piece of butcher-block paper (Figure 3.7). Students bring their community knowledge to the table as they illustrate and write about landmarks they know best. Those who live near the Family Dollar store or the Kentucky Fried Chicken, for example, know the route from their homes, so they are experts at creating that part of the map—further opportunities for children to blend community knowledge with conventions of schooling.

Phone Calls

Before their day ends on the first day of school, Janice and Carmen make phone calls to every family. Although notes, email, Twitter, and text messages can be effective forms of communication, hearing the teacher's voice seems to make all the difference in initiating positive and lasting relationships.

Through the phone calls, Janice and Carmen share something positive from each child's first day. They ask about families' goals for their children and what the

Figure 3.6. Writing Ideas List

When I went to Charleston to see my brother.
When somebody pushed me.
When I had a accident.
I like to go to my aunt's home.
When I went to the beach.
I love to go to the park.
I love to go to Burger King.
When my mom had a baby.
When my hand got stuck in the car.

After choosing a topic, thinking about imagery:
What do you hear?

I hear my mom say, "I Love you" in my ear."
My mom said it soft.
My mom said, "I love you boy. You look good boy to me."
She said, "I love my sweet little baby boy."
I love you mom and dad too. You look sweet to me baby boy.

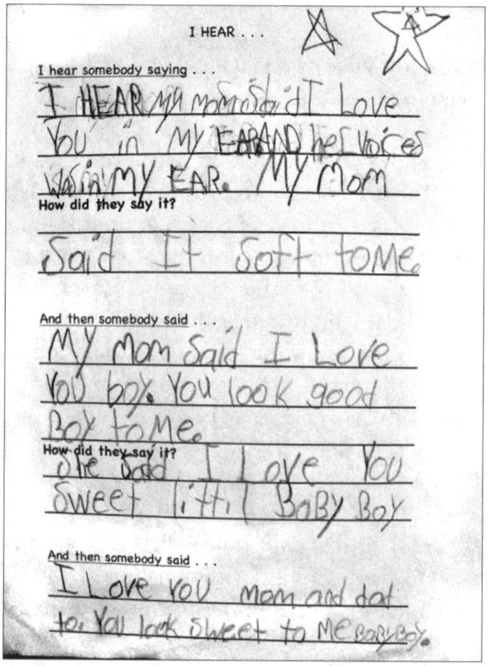

Figure 3.7. Community Map

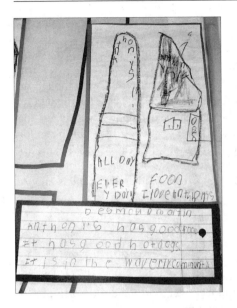

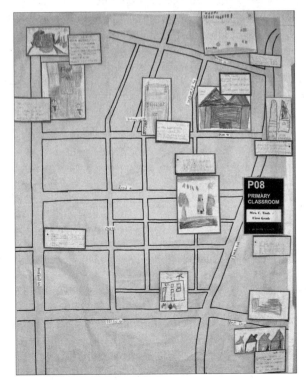

families cherish about them. Their purpose is to communicate to families that they matter, their views matter, and that they are *relevant* to the classroom.

Parents are often surprised at these calls. Carmen tells about phoning the mother of 5-year-old Khalil to share how much she "loved his mind." She said to Khalil's mother: "I can already tell that he is going to be a joy to teach. He sat at my feet today and listened intently as I read. He seems very eager to learn." Khalil's mother was pleasantly surprised. She told Carmen that, even though she had never received negative calls from Khalil's teachers, when she heard that Carmen was on the other end of the line, she thought he had done something wrong. These first day phone calls helped to dispel that expectation and establish comfort in communication that would continue throughout the year. Mrs. Williams, the mother of 1st-grader Javon, told Carmen, "You are the only teacher that made me feel comfortable calling you. I like that we talk to each other. Every call is important to me."

"TOMORROW'S PROMISE"

Standing in the empty room at the beginning of the year, we think about building a space where students see, hear, and feel their worth and the worth of people in the larger society, where the classroom becomes a home away from home, where a sense of family belonging and communal responsibility is established, and where a collective humanity is embraced. Critical to making this happen is looking through students' and families' eyes. When they walk into the classroom and experience the first week's activities, will they see themselves and their communities depicted in positive ways? Will they see the normalization of people, languages, and histories typically omitted or marginalized? Will they feel that they are loved and cared for? Will they know that their stories matter and that issues of justice will be acted on here? Janice's words captured the essence of this spirit as she described the walk toward her classroom:

> Walking down the primary wing, we know we are getting close to some of the community's treasures, the children of room 39. The colorful walls and the voices of 6- and 7-year-old learners capture any visitor's heart. The four walls hold a family of learners and tomorrow's promise. The children learn from the first day of school that they are readers and writers, that they and their families are brilliant, and that we are a family of learners supporting each other. The print-rich walls reflect their community, a neighborhood chant, or a familiar rap. If you listen closely, you may hear the students whispering parts of their newly learned class chant, "I'm a boundless scholar," as they make their way through the first days of school. When you leave room 39, it will remain dear to your heart. The children will have loved and taught you each moment they are learning and growing.

CHAPTER 4

Musical Literacies in the Culturally Relevant Classroom

> I can tell students that I believe in them and that they are important. But music—music can build positive self-image, self-esteem, and self-love. Music is a part of their everyday lives and their history. They listen to it and don't even realize they are internalizing it as a part of who they are. School doesn't always provide that piece with regard to Black histories. So, throughout the day I play music that gives life to that vision. —Carmen

In Janice and Carmen's classrooms, each morning begins with music and it filters throughout the day. The sounds of jazz, rhythm and blues (R&B), music from West Africa, or hip-hop greet the children as they enter. The children hear music as they work at their seats, settle in after recess, and prepare to go home.

In this chapter, we share musical literacy practices developed to broaden what counts as literacy; spark heritage, social justice, and literacy lessons; and teach students that literacy is *for them, by them,* and *about them.* Although these practices were helpful in building literacy skills, they were powerful because they built on the cultural wealth of communities and histories often left out of the canon. Through these musical literacies, we worked to convey that African and African American musical heritage reflect literary genres "just as relevant and worthy of study as [that] of students whose cultural identities are traditionally represented in classroom literature" (Kelly, 2013, p. 53).

We share musical literacies offering a strong caveat that is discussed further in the "Continuing to Grow" section of this chapter: It is easy to trivialize musical literacy by using it purely to "entice students into learning some of the same old information [we] have been teaching for years" (Ladson-Billings, 2017, p. 152) or as "bait and switch for content that is [considered] more important" (Lyiscott, 2017a). There are certainly elements of teaching conventional skills through music in our examples. The children were drawn to school-based literacy conventions through music. However, we also emphasize the power of musical literacies to broaden students' knowledge of who matters in the history of the world, and affirm hip-hop and other musical genres as legitimate literary texts and as entrées into critically conscious thinking.

MUSICAL LITERACIES AND HISTORIES IN CARMEN'S CLASSROOM

It was cool that we could listen to [Daniel D.] in class. I didn't know that
African Americans could do this kind of stuff like playing the violin and hip-
hop together. My 3rd-grade teacher played jazz, but not this kind of stuff.
—Brion, 2nd-grader

Carmen often opens the year with the music of saxophonist Dante Lewis because
he is an African American musician from the students' hometown. Carmen wants
students to see that he is their reality and potential—talented, beautiful, and successful. She loves that his music reflects many musical aspects of African American culture through its focus on gospel, hip-hop, and rhythm and blues.

Carmen also introduces hip-hop violinist Daniel D. early in the year. The students' curiosity about a musician from their state never fails to motivate them
to research his life and music. Carmen pulls up his website (www.danieldmusic.
com/) on the Smartboard for all to see, placing his genius front and center. The
students soon feel like they know him personally. They love his sound and connect
to his youth and musical vibe. Carmen situates his music in a history of jazz and
blues that goes back to its New Orleans and African roots.

With these introductions to local musicians, Carmen sets a musical tone in
her classroom. This paves the way for further explorations through music throughout the year.

Musical Connections, History, and Language

The first year that Carmen decided to use music as an organizing theme, she initiated it with the book described in Chapter 3, *When I Was a Little Girl.* Among
other aspects of her life, the book introduced the children to music loved by Carmen and her father, mother, and aunt. As a result, the Temptations, Grover Washington, Gladys Knight and the Pips, Teddy Pendergrass, and Al Green became a
part of the classroom's shared musical and historical knowledge. Carmen played
their music regularly, talked about their histories, and built from those musicians
to acquaint the children with other blues, jazz, and R&B greats. In the process, she
made connections between her family and the musical heritage that her students
would study through the year:

> I explain to the children that I play jazz because my dad played it for me. He
> broadened my musical world. I want the children to know that music they
> hear today stands on the shoulders of great Black musicians.

These personal musical connections led Carmen to a range of read-alouds
(see suggestions in text box). The use of trade books allowed her to expand students' knowledge about musical histories while expanding their vocabularies and
strengthening their skills as readers. As she read aloud, Carmen guided students

> ### Children's Books About African American Musical Heritage
>
> Andrews, T. (2015). *Trombone Shorty*
> Briere-Haquet, A. (2017). *Nina: Jazz Legend and Civil Rights Activist*
> Dillon, L. & Dillon, D. (2007). *Jazz on a Saturday Night*
> Engle, E. (2015). *Drum Dream Girl: How One Girl's Courage Changed Music*
> Giovanni, N. (2008). *Hip Hop Speaks to Children*
> Golio, G. (2017). *Strange Fruit: Billie Holiday and the Power of a Protest Song*
> Grimes, N. (2017). *One Last Word: Wisdom from the Harlem Renaissance*
> Hill, L. C. (2013). *When the Beat Was Born: DJ Kool Herc and the Creation of Hip Hop*
> Marsalis, W. (2012). *Squeak, Rumble, Whomp! Whomp! Whomp! A Sonic Adventure*
> Mahin, M. (2017). *Muddy: The Story of Blues Legend Muddy Waters*
> Pinkney, A. D. (2006). *Duke Ellington*
> Pinkney, A. D. (2015). *Rhythm Ride: A Road Trip Through the Motown Sound*
> Pinkney, A. D. (2013). *Martin & Mahalia: His Words, Her Song*
> Powell, P. H. (2014). *Josephine: The Dazzling Life of Josephine Baker*
> Ryan, P. M. & Selznick, B. (2002). *When Marian Sang: The True Recital of Marian Anderson*
> Watson, R. (2012). *Harlem's Little Blackbird: The Story of Florence Mills*
> Weatherford, C. B. (2017). *The Legendary Miss Lena Horne*
> Weatherford, C. B. (2008). *Before John Was a Jazz Giant: A Song of John Coltrane*

to notice the authors' use of language: "Let's read that sentence again. Listen for words that help you hear and see and feel the music and the people who are making and enjoying the music." For example, they created a large chart of words from the picture book *Jazz on a Saturday Night* (Dillon & Dillon, 2006), highlighting words like *absolutely*, *gulp*, *brave*, and *applause*. From *Ella Fitzgerald* (Pinkney, 2002), they added words and phrases such as *virtuosa*, *quiet as a whisper*, *soft as a cricket*, *perfectionist*, and *orchestra*. Because Carmen encouraged the students to use these words and phrases in their writing, the books provided important resources as well as history and language lessons.

"My Girl"

When I Was a Little Girl also prompted students' connections to Carmen's favorite childhood song, "My Girl." When she came to the page that read, "When I was a little girl, I loved the song 'My Girl,'" she heard comments like, "My grandmama loves that song, too!" The children particularly loved the photo of Carmen with arms raised in the air, snapping her fingers: "We would throw our hands in the air, snap our fingers, and say, 'THAT'S MY SONG!'" Children like Terrence shared their connections, calling out, "My mom says that, too!"

To capitalize on the enthusiasm for "My Girl," Susi and the children created a book using its lyrics. Like every other book they created, each page was developed as a PowerPoint slide, printed, and coil-bound with copies placed in baskets around the room and at the listening center with electronic versions available on the computer.

In addition to using "My Girl" to get to know her students and introduce them to an era of music, it was easy to connect it to skills required by the district pacing guide. For example, lessons about contractions were effortlessly woven into talk about lyrics like "I've got sunshine, on a cloudy day. When it's cold outside, I've got the month of May." Students grew in their understanding of reading fluency as Carmen pointed out their fluid reading of the familiar text: "Listen to how your reading flows!" They also learned vocabulary, sentence structure, and high-frequency words while reading a book that they loved, that they could read, and that connected them to their teacher, music, and history.

"My Girl" was powerful in the way it engaged readers who had been disenfranchised from other texts. First-grader Ileka is a case in point. She seldom connected with books and was always on the move, sometimes hanging upside down from her seat or walking around the room rarely focused on assigned tasks. "She wasn't a behavior problem," Carmen explained. "She was just unfocused. I had to find ways to reach her." When Ileka did sit down for a reading conference, she often put her finger on a word, looked at Carmen, and smiled without saying anything. But when Carmen introduced "My Girl," Ileka was the first student at the listening center pointing to the lyrics as she sang along to the Temptations' recording, reading it over and over. Ileka was similarly engaged when Carmen used the book for small- and large-group instruction: "I didn't have to tell her to focus; I just had to teach and she was willing to learn." With Carmen's instruction, Ileka soon began transferring literacy skills learned from "My Girl" to other texts. Most important, she began to exhibit confidence and focus as a reader and was developing knowledge about musical histories.

Music We Love!

After "My Girl," Carmen engaged the children in creating a book about *their* musical favorites. Each child created a page about a favorite song. Carmen began by drafting her own writing in front of the class setting up a format to ensure writing success during the first weeks of 1st grade. She talked through her writing choices (modeling the thought processes of a writer) as she demonstrated on the whiteboard (Figure 4.1). Using interactive writing techniques (McCarrier, Pinnell, & Fountas, 1999), Carmen invited the children to write letters or parts of words they knew as they created her draft together:

> I'll start by introducing myself: *My name is Mrs. Tisdale.* How do I write the word *My*? Say it with me—*my*. Does it begin like anyone's name we know? Yes, it starts just like Makayla's name. Find Makayla's picture on the alphabet wall. The letter above it is an M. M for *Makayla* and M for *my*. Makayla, would you write the letter M in my sentence?

Figure 4.1. Carmen's Demonstration of the Format for *Music We Love!* and Drafts of Student Pages

My favorite song is "My Girl." I like it because it has a cool sound.

My favorite song is Apple Bottem jeans. I like it because I like to step.

My favorite Song is Wocka Flocka. because I like it makes me dance.

Then the students generated a list of *their* favorite songs as Carmen wrote them on the board next to their names and they began drafting their pages following Carmen's format (Figure 4.1). As they worked, Carmen met with students in one-to-one writing conferences to help them think through spelling, sentence structure, spacing, letter formation, and punctuation. On subsequent days, Carmen demonstrated how to work toward final, publishable work.

The predictable nature of the text made it possible for 1st-grade writers to feel confident and successful. Marcus is a perfect example. His typical response to writing assignments was to look at other students' papers, get frustrated, and cry, protesting, "I can't do it!" The only time he could be urged to write was when Carmen pulled her chair next to him and talked him through each step. However, with the opportunity to write about music he loved and the reassuring structure of an established format, Marcus wrote with a sense of accomplishment and no tears. He still needed a lot of support, but he was building the confidence necessary to take risks as a writer.

The students met with Susi to type their text on PowerPoint slides. Photos were added, pages were compiled, and the book *Music We Love!* was born. Projecting the book onto the Smartboard, Carmen used it for whole-class instruction. She invited the children to read with her, celebrating their musical choices. Familiarity with pages that they had produced and the predictable text allowed them to hear and practice smooth and expressive reading. This laid the groundwork for teaching everything from left-to-right directionality and one-to-one correspondence to high-frequency words, vocabulary, and making analogies between words in *Music We Love!* and words in other contexts: "If you can read *name*—as in *My name is*—then you can read *same, game, tame, fame.*"

Music We Love! also gave Carmen opportunities to better understand the children's needs as readers and writers. For example, she learned that Ileka read high-frequency words in *Music We Love!* but did not transfer that knowledge to trade books. So Carmen worked one to one with Ileka to demonstrate how to use that knowledge to read other texts.

Finally, *Music We Love!* provided an opportunity to connect with families, engender family talk about music, and support literacy learning at home. Carmen and Susi created take-home versions of the book—stapled-together pages, half the size of the classroom books. In take-home packets, they included suggestions for families to use as they enjoyed the book together:

- Read *Music We Love!* together: You can alternate reading pages or read them at the same time. This will help your child develop reading fluency (smooth, not choppy, reading).
- Talk about the songs in the book: What do you know about them? Share music you love; share memories from your life that connect you to music.
- After enjoying the book together, help your child identify words in it: "Let's find the word *Ileka*." "How many times can we find the word *because*?" "Let's find it in other texts (books, websites, and so forth)."
- Create new words using familiar patterns from *Music We Love!* For example, you can say to your child, "If you can read *My name is*, you know the word *name*. If you can read *name*, you can write and read other words that have the same pattern. Let's write some words" (*same, came, frame*, and so on).

After taking the books and suggested activities home, the students came back to school and shared their families' musical memories during gathering time (simultaneously addressing listening and speaking standards) and wrote about their families' musical favorites in their daily journals.

Hand Jives

Hand jives or handclapping rhymes have a long history in African oral traditions and rhythms. *Likwata*, for example, is an East African term for the clapping of hands, and *lipapali* from South Africa means "play songs." Handed down through centuries and across oceans, these rhymes and motions played a huge role in the students' lives, particularly for the girls. On the playground, they could regularly be seen initiating the complex clapping movements and verbal poetry. Taking signals from one another, they began slowly and then clapped faster and faster, laughing when one of them stumbled, then picking up where they left off.

Noticing their engagement, Carmen decided to use hand jives to continue the focus on musical literacies. She started with "Miss Mary Mack," which was familiar to many of the children. Because "Miss Mary Mack" was introduced as a legitimate form of classroom literacy, the boys—who didn't engage in handclapping rhymes on the playground—were just as excited as the girls to participate in singing and clapping together.

Carmen, Susi, and the children created a *Miss Mary Mack* book which included the rhyme and the children's illustrations. They posted the words to "Miss

Figure 4.2. "Miss Mary Mack" and Other Class-Made Books Used in the Word Study Area

Mary Mack" on the classroom walls. The children eagerly sought the books for independent reading or when they chose to "Read the Room" as an independent literacy option (walking around the classroom reading poems, song lyrics, word charts, and other texts displayed on the walls).

As the children gained familiarity with the written word patterns in *Miss Mary Mack,* Carmen helped them use those patterns to read new words: "If you can read *Mack*, you can read other words with the same pattern (*tack, stack, Jack*)." They learned about initial consonants by creating lists of words that start like *Mack* and *Mary* and *Miss.* They used the phrase *all dressed in black* to generate words with *bl-* blends, a requirement in the district pacing guide and they worked with "Miss Mary Mack" words at the word study center (Figure 4.2).

"Black History Is Our History"

After the successful use of music during the first months of school, Carmen decided to develop a musical hook that would allow her to teach beyond the typical focus on a few Black leaders only during Black History Month. This led to commissioning her brother, Chop Dezol, to write the "Black History Is Our History" rap. She explained:

I thought about the children's pages in *Music We Love!* Overwhelmingly, they showed their love of rap. So, I reached out to my brother, who is known in the music business as hip-hop artist and mentor Chop Dezol. We had talked about how important it was to use his talent to make a difference for children and this was a way to do that. So he wrote "Black History Is Our History" and made a recording to use in class.

"Black History Is Our History" (Dezol, 2010; see References for a link to download the song) introduces African American genius to the children as the lyrics include the names and accomplishments of scientists, activists, inventors, authors, composers, leaders of nations, performers, television pioneers, and CEOs of major corporations. Carmen uses the song no matter the demographic of her classroom, emphasizing that Black history is not just for Black History Month. It is American history; it is world history—all year long.

Carmen invites the children into the rap by playing it for several days as they enter the room. The beat and the hook (repeated refrain) grab their attention:

Hop to the left, hop to the right
Walk it in a circle if learning's what you like
Hold up, wait a minute, let me put some knowledge in it. (Dezol, 2010)

Then Carmen teaches the verses that name Black contributors to the world's knowledge: "Black history is our history, it's time to represent. Like Harriet Tubman, the Underground Railroad; Rosa Parks, sometimes you gotta say no." The first year the song was introduced, Carmen, Susi, and the children used the lyrics to create another book, illustrated with photos of the students dancing to the song.

Already used pedagogically with middle and high school students (Hill, 2009; Stovall, 2006), hip-hop was a perfect link to history and literacy for Carmen's 1st-graders. Several years later, Bettina Love (2015) wrote a now-well-known article about hip-hop–based education as important for "our youngest learners" (p. 108)—powerful in promoting cognitive, storytelling, and language skills. In Carmen's classroom, "Black History Is Our History" does just that. While deepening their acquaintance with Black genius, the students learn about rap as a form of art and literacy that can "hold its intellectual own within traditional academic spaces" (p. 13).

Research and writing. Carmen also uses "Black History Is Our History" as an entrée into students' research into history. With the song as a basis, Carmen fills baskets with books about Black contributors to the world's knowledge and the classroom becomes a research zone. Carmen teaches the children to use the library and websites to access information. They write letters to contemporary figures and interview their own family and community members, asking questions such as: Who are the most important African Americans to you? What can you teach me about them? Why is it important to learn about African American history?

> ### Resources for Learning About African and African American Contributors to the World's Knowledge
>
> Abdul-Jabbar, K. (2013). *What Color Is My World: The Lost History of African American Inventors*
>
> Clarke, J. H. (1993). *African People in World History*
>
> Cook, M. (2012). *Our Children Can Soar*
>
> Gates, H. L. & West, C. (2002). *The African American Century: How Black Americans Have Shaped Our Country*
>
> Hansen, J. (2004). *African Princess: The Amazing Lives of Africa's Royal Women*
>
> Hudson, W. (2003). *Books of Black Heroes: Scientists, Healers, and Inventors*
>
> Pinkney, A. D. & Pinkney, B. (2012). *Hand in Hand: Ten Black Men Who Changed America*
>
> Smith, J. C. (2012). *Black Firsts: 4,000 Ground-Breaking and Pioneering Historical Events*
>
> Stewart, J. (1998). *1001 Things Everyone Should Know About African American History*
>
> Sullivan, O. R. (2012). *Black Stars: African American Inventors*

Using a writers workshop approach (Ray, 2001)—brainstorming, drafting, editing, rewriting, publishing—the children use their research to create their own books. An example is provided in Figure 4.3 of several pages from Sameka's research about Madam C. J. Walker. Carmen teaches minilessons and conducts one-to-one conferences to help students build further expertise with nonfiction writing, sentence structure, spelling strategies, details, and vocabulary. Every year, the books become a part of the classroom library and are read and reread throughout the year.

The opportunity to build from "Black History Is Our History" to initiate research and write about African Americans has "deep impact, significant relevance, and strong staying power" (Jenkins, 2013, p. 15) for the students. Two examples stand out in the stories of 1st-grader Jamon and 2nd-grader Brion.

Jamon excelled as a reader and writer, but he was disenfranchised from almost everything in the classroom. Carmen worried about him:

> Jamon never seemed happy. He was smart as a whip and worked far above grade level, but he didn't get excited about anything. Sometimes he would get angry in a way that seemed scary for a child that age, fighting mad.
> He gave me stellar work on assignments, but he usually only participated verbally if I asked him directly. I constantly worried about him because he was clearly not enjoying 1st grade.

When Jamon worked on his Black history project, however, his attitude changed completely. He researched radio personality and activist Tom Joyner.

Figure 4.3. Excerpts from Biography of Madam C. J. Walker

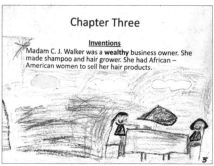
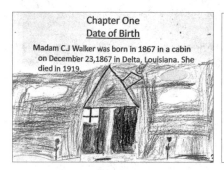
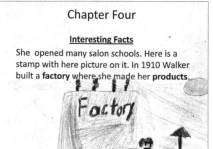

Jamon was excited to work with a small research group and send an email to Tom Joyner. One morning, Carmen opened her email and there was Tom Joyner's name: "Jamon, look! Tom Joyner wrote you back!" When Jamon saw the email, Carmen saw a smile she rarely witnessed.

The connection between Jamon's deep engagement with a topic that was meaningful to him and the opportunity to build heritage knowledge is significant. Studies show that academic disenfranchisement, particularly when exhibited by African American boys, often stems from a Eurocentric curriculum that renders students of color invisible or fails to challenge or engage them intellectually (Kirkland, 2016a; Tatum, 2009). The opportunity to research Black male genius provided the culturally relevant motivation that Jamon needed to use his brilliance to excel.

Brion was similarly enthusiastic about his research into the life of Thurgood Marshall. Several years after he was in Carmen's class, his grandmother, Ms. Jenkins, explained the project's staying power:

> One of the things he still really likes to talk about is Thurgood Marshall. He *wanted* to do that research. He just ran with the judge thing. He wanted to play "judge." He wanted to go to school to be a judge.

Brion also remembered how the project helped him develop belief in his own potential:

> The project was awesome. I had a presentation. It was a wax museum. You pressed a button and I spoke about Thurgood Marshall. I learned how he did things in the courtroom. It made me think I could be a judge, too, that I could just have the belief.

Social justice teaching. Building on the social justice foundation initiated during the first week of school, Carmen also uses "Black History Is Our History" to engage students in further critical consciousness building. For example, she uses the song to help the students connect Dr. King's dream to President Barack Obama's presidency, and then to the students' responsibility to take action for change. "Remember the words from our Black history rap?" she asks and then recites an excerpt with them: "'It started from a dream and the dream became Barack, now President Obama.' Well, now it's not just Dr. King and it's not just President Obama; it's you and me who are a part of the dream." This creates openings to discuss issues of the day. Then Carmen asks the children to write new goals for keeping the dream of justice alive. As they did during the first weeks of school, the students make plans for meeting their goals and report back to the class about the success of their efforts.

"Black History Is Our History" lives on. Many of Carmen's students teach "Black History Is Our History" to their younger brothers and sisters. As a result, siblings who enter Carmen's classroom in subsequent years have an immediate connection to her. During school assemblies when Carmen's class sings the song, students from previous years sing along, reflecting their shared history and identification with the larger community. Students teach the rap to their parents and grandparents, who sing it with Carmen at family literacy evenings. But the experience goes far beyond just singing a favorite song. It brings a sense of validation and affirmation. Brion's grandmother, Ms. Jenkins, explained:

> I just think that sometimes children don't know that we come from kings and queens. They have no idea we [invented] things. So they don't have any ownership—self-worth. [They think], "No one else has done anything, so why should I?" I really appreciate that you integrated this as a part of the learning process.

DRUMS, SWAG, OUR BROTHAS, OUR HEARTS:
JANICE'S SCHOLARS CONNECTING THROUGH MUSIC

> You came to the hospital and taught me "I Can Read Swag." You were so loud;
> you thought you were Soulja Boy! —James, 1st-grader

At the beginning of her second year of teaching, Janice worried that her students did not see literate futures for themselves. She wanted to show them that literacy was already a part of their lives and that they could use that knowledge to continue to grow as readers and writers. That year, she began using music in new ways.

"I Can Read Swag"

During the first weeks of school, Janice noticed that her students were singing a particular song on the playground—"Pretty Boy Swag" (Soulja Boy, 2010). Picking up on their engagement with the song, she wrote new lyrics to the familiar rhythm and introduced "I Can Read Swag" to her class:

> Learning, learning, learning, learning, learning, learning, learning.
> This—right here—is my—book!
> Watch—me—read—the pages—look!
> Every-body pay attention.
> This, right here, is my—
> I can read swag—read!
> I can read swag—read!

With this refrain, the children knew immediately that this was their song. They learned it quickly and soon they were singing it quietly as they worked at their seats or as they walked to lunch: "Get out the wayyyy, smart kids coming through. I'm tryin' to find a book that I can show you." They taught "Swag" to friends in Carmen's classroom. They danced to it.

Swag, the Book. Janice created a book using the lyrics to "Swag" (Figure 4.4). Through it, she taught and celebrated the students as readers. Using "Swag" in bound copies and projected on the Smartboard, Janice used it for large- and small-group work and the children read it during independent reading time. In the process Janice was able to show students that a familiar musical text was a form of literacy. The 1st-graders read "Swag" to their 3rd-grade book buddies. They transferred knowledge learned through "Swag" to other texts, pointing out words as they walked down the halls or read other books: "Look, that word is just like in 'Swag'!" Janice constantly reinforced their excitement as they found words from "Swag" everywhere: "Oh my goodness, I see a word we know!"

Figure 4.4. Using "I Can Read Swag" for Read-Alouds, Projected on the Smartboard, for Independent Reading

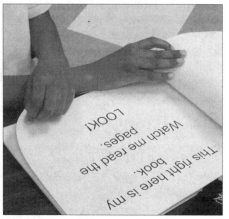

Impact. One of the most vivid illustrations of the impact of "Swag" came from a 1st grader named James. James was home- or hospital-bound most of his 1st-grade year. Janice brought a copy of "I Can Read Swag" to her first meeting with him in the hospital. She sat on the edge of his bed, opened "Swag," and started singing and pointing to words. James was hesitant, but soon he began reading along. Although, as a reader, he was just beginning to identify letters and a few words, within a few minutes, he could read "Swag"'s refrain. When Janice left that day, James knew success as a reader and was already developing a loving relationship with his teacher. Several years later, James remembered Janice's spirit as she introduced him to "Swag":

"You came to the hospital and taught me 'I Can Read Swag.' You were so loud, you thought you were Soulja Boy!" His mother also shared memories of the power of "Swag" and of Janice as a teacher:

> You started singing it loud and there was James hooked up to this IV machine, a lot of medicine running through him and he was looking like, "Is she kidding?" You put the book down in front of him and he was like, "Okay, I can do this." Because of that book, he knew he could read and when he was able to go to school he had a connection to the rest of the class.

Caveat: "Swag" isn't the point; knowing your students is. When we share "Swag" stories at professional conferences, teachers inevitably ask for a recording of the song. However, that misses the point. Asking for a recording of "Swag" is like asking for a scripted program or a workbook. The power of "Swag" was not that it was a cute song to teach letters and sounds, but that it (1) captured the musical interests of a group of children in a specific moment in time, (2) showed the children that a familiar musical genre was legitimate literary text, and (3) demonstrated to the children that there was much that they could easily read and write.

Once again, Janice did not essentialize her students by assuming they would be interested in rap just because they were African American. She learned about music they loved by talking with them, spending time in homes and communities, listening to their radio stations, and watching YouTube videos of songs the children talked about. "If you make them feel comfortable enough at school," she said, "they'll start singing songs they love out of nowhere. I just pay attention."

Our Brothas, Our Hearts

Janice rejoiced in and worried about all of her students, but she knew that her African American boys would face a particular kind of unearned discrimination as they grew into young men (Howard, 2014; Tatum, 2009). She could see that many people, including educators, already saw them as less capable than their White peers. Janice wanted her boys to see themselves for what they were—smart, capable, and caring—so the first time she heard the song "Brotha" by Angie Stone (2006), she knew she had to introduce it to her class. Janice felt that the song needed little explanation to the children, so she let it speak for itself:

> That's how good the song is. I didn't have to say anything. *He is my king*—so I could say to my boys, "You guys are my kings." You're strong, you're smart, you're patient. The song validates the things that I told them they are—*I want you to know that, I'm here for you.*

"Brotha"'s creator is Angie Stone, an artist who grew up in the neighborhood where many of the students lived. Many of the children recognized it as a family favorite so it was not just the boys who wanted this song on repeat. The girls were moved by it too. "Brotha" helped Janice set an important tone that, instead of pitting boys and girls against one another, brought them together.

"Just for Today"

One year, Janice introduced India Arie's (2016) song "Just for Today" to her 1st graders. She knew that she wouldn't be able to teach anything until the children knew they were valued. She felt that this song communicated just the right message: "I saw it as something that would let my students know that we all feel vulnerable at times, but that we are strong and capable."

Janice described how, within a few hours after playing the song, the children's voices were completely tuned in to the beat and flow of the words. She often played the song in the background as they worked. She used the lyrics to talk about the children's value to the world and how no one has all the answers to our questions but we have to keep asking and seeking answers. Janice wanted them to have confidence in and be able to stand up for their abilities. The message filled the classroom with lyrics like "I won't let it stand in the way, I know what I must do . . . and it's time for me to show and prove."

CONTINUING TO GROW

Of all the genres used to teach in culturally relevant ways, musical literacies hold some of the greatest joys as well as the greatest potential pitfalls. When teachers asked for copies of "I Can Read Swag," it was an important wakeup call for us. It let us know that our work could be interpreted at a very surface level, dissolving into pedagogical cuteness: Aren't they cute rapping about reading? We realized how easily people could walk away from our presentations only remembering our use of musical literacies to teach skills.

So, although we see Carmen and Janice's students empowered as readers and writers as they come to understand music as a literary genre with voice, convention, text, and language (Duncan-Andrade & Morrell, 2008), we know that our teaching also helped them understand music as rooted in history and affirmation. However, there is much more we can do. We can grow our teaching by exploring music from a more critical stance and deepening the historical connections. Some possibilities include engaging students in studying the following:

- The history of handclap rhymes, taking them back to African and African Diaspora roots.
- Musical genres—spirituals, jazz, blues, hip-hop—as aligned with sociopolitical histories: resistance, reconstruction, Jim Crow, the Harlem Renaissance, civil rights, and the #BlackLivesMatter movement (McCormack, 2018).

- The lives and musical goals of musicians whose work is anchored in justice movements.
- Students' own musical compositions as a way to speak to issues of today
- African American, Latinx, Native American, and Asian musical forms and historic commonalities that link them to African and African Diaspora influences.
- Critical examinations of musical genres to understand how music can uplift but can also reproduce "discourses that marginalize members of our communities" (Paris & Alim, 2017, p. 11), for example, learning to identify and speak back to elements of homophobia, misogyny, and racism that may be found in some music.

Finally, if you are not comfortable with particular musical literacies that push curriculum beyond the Eurocentric canon, make yourself knowledgeable by studying histories, artists, musical movements, and connections to African and African Diaspora roots. Reject inauthenticity by enlisting the help of musicians and other experts who *are* knowledgeable about musical styles and genres. Invite them into your classroom to teach you and your students as learners together.

"MUSIC HELPS US SAY, 'WE ARE ALL IN THIS TOGETHER'"

There is no "How do I teach this?" The music and the words either strike a chord for you and your students or they don't. You know when you've struck the right chord. —Janice

At its core, music was a way for Janice, Carmen, their students, and students' families to connect with one another. It was one of the heartstrings that Janice talked about in Chapter 3. Using musical literacies, it was possible to strike chords that built children's belief in themselves as knowledgeable, capable contributors to the world and to appreciate contributions beyond their immediate worlds. Janice summed up the essence of the experience:

No matter where we are, when my students and I hear our songs, we will be reminded of each other and of the courage and confidence we developed to be able to say that news or media cannot define who you are or who you will become. You will be leaders, kind and attentive fathers and mothers, smart contributors to the world. Music helps us say we are all in this together, learning and growing as a family.

CHAPTER 5

Oral Histories
Preserving Community Stories

That book they made about me, it was just amazing. I can't believe these kids actually remembered what I said and put it in writing. I told them how [our community] was a family-oriented place where everybody looked out for one another and they listened to that. I told them that we have so many young people that's doing so good in this world that came out of this community and the kids remember those things. That book they made about me was really inspiring. —Ms. Myers, community elder

Engaging 1st-graders in collecting oral histories from community elders resulted in some of our most powerful culturally relevant and humanizing teaching. This chapter focuses on those experiences as the students developed intergenerational texts by interviewing and then creating books about elders. We wanted students to know that they had "something to say about [their] community" (Kinloch, 2010, p. 91) and that they could grow in literacy proficiency, cultural competence, and critical consciousness as they honored and learned from elders.

The community in which Janice and Carmen's students lived during this oral history work (a grouping of neighborhoods that are part of a larger city) reflects a rich heritage of African American scientists, educators, artisans, politicians, physicians, civil rights leaders, attorneys, teachers, photographers, entrepreneurs, railroaders, musicians, and sports figures. From the 1920s through the 1960s, a library, shops, law offices, hotels, churches, restaurants, and a hospital thrived. A local hotel was a center for civil rights activities of the 1950s and 1960s and a stopover for entertainer-activists like Ruby Dee, Ossie Davis, and Jackie Wilson.

By the time Janice and Carmen's 1st-graders studied the community, however, White-dominated media had successfully propagated profiles that emphasized poverty, crime, gang presence, and underemployment. Dominant narratives made no mention of the area's strengths or heritage. Blame for any decline in the community was typically placed on its residents rather than on racist structures that had long ensured there would be a decrease in prosperity: the enduring impact of enslavement, Black Codes, Jim Crow, and the displacement of families and businesses resulting from gentrification. There was no mention of the community's strengths and history in state or local school curricula. As Carmen explained, the history was virtually unspoken:

Nobody ever told me or our students that their school was nestled in a community that was on the National Register of Historic Places. Once I was introduced to the history, I was inspired to learn more. I wanted to show my students that they had strong shoulders to stand on.

As a result, we began to think about how we might involve the children in seeking what Janice calls "hidden truths" to liberate them from the dominant narratives. At a time when gentrification was tearing apart their neighborhoods, we wanted students to learn from the wisdom of elders who helped shape those communities.

COLLECTING HISTORIES

The oral histories collected by Janice and Carmen's students were initially inspired by Valerie Kinloch's (2010) work with high school students who documented, narrated, and critiqued the gentrification of their Harlem neighborhoods. This sparked the idea for us to engage Janice and Carmen's 1st-graders in learning about and preserving the histories of their communities. The work was also informed by local teacher Edward Hill, whose 3rd-graders collected and analyzed observational and interview data as they conducted a study of local barbershops to gain deeper understandings about "the strengths of the Black community" (Boutte & Hill, 2006, p. 149).

Over the course of a school year, Janice and Carmen's students interviewed a range of community elders: a school board member, local attorney, school custodian, retired kindergarten teacher, one of the first African American nurses at the local VA hospital, the school's principal, and the owner of a community barbershop that had been located on a corner near the school for 75 years. Each community member described a proud legacy of growing up in the neighborhoods where the students lived. The children's writing and illustrations based on the interviews became the foundation for books created to honor each community member. The collection of books became the students' *Preserving Our Community Stories* series.

Preparation: First, We Needed to Learn

As teachers, we began by steeping ourselves in the history of the community. This meant seeking accurate scholarship (King & Swartz, 2016) by critically reading accounts of community history in books and on websites. For each account, we asked who was telling the story (insiders? outsiders?) and whose voices were heard and not heard. Then we sought unheard accounts by talking to people within the community.

Approached in this way, each person we asked and each document we accessed led us to further resources. Susi visited the "Wall of Fame," a park that honored community members with photos and short biographies posted on brick fence posts. Carmen and Janice talked to family members of their students and people in local churches and places of business. Susi learned from people at the community's health clinic, and the community wellness center, and from historian Dr. Bobby Donaldson from the Center for Civil Rights History and Research at the University of South Carolina.

Teaching About Preservation and Gentrification

Preparing to introduce the idea of oral histories to the students, we wanted to use our research to go further than merely teaching students how to conduct interviews. This was an important opportunity to build students' critical consciousness. We wanted them to understand why their neighborhoods should be revered and respected, as well as oppressive practices that led to the erasure of the community's rich history from dominant narratives. So, we engaged them in discussions about gentrification, a process familiar to the children as they watched the dislocation of families and friends and worried about their own eventual displacement.

We began by discussing the community's historical significance. Then we taught the terms *gentrification* and *preservation*. We discussed the process of gentrification and the students' feelings about it. We talked about actions the children could take to preserve stories that would be lost as people were displaced. To frame the children's discussions, we posed guiding questions:

- What do you notice that is happening in your community (apartments being torn down, people moving)?
- What will remain the same? What will be different?
- Will people come back? Why? Why not?
- How do you feel about this?
- What should we preserve from the community before more families move away?

Preparing to Conduct Interviews

To further prepare students, we worked with them to generate interview questions. We asked them: What do you want to know about the community and its history? What stories should we ask our guests to tell? What can they teach us about the community and its history? Janice's students generated questions together as she wrote them on a piece of chart paper. In Carmen's class, the students drafted questions in their journals, shared them with partners, and gave one another feedback for refining or clarifying the questions. Then they shared their questions aloud as Carmen typed and projected them on the Smartboard.

Many of the questions came straight from the hearts and minds of 6-year-olds, questions about music, food, and what people liked to do when they were children. Other questions were clear evidence that our discussions about history, gentrification, and preservation played an important role in extending the students' reach:

- Where did you grow up in our community? What house did you grow up in? Is it still there? Why? Why not?
- Did your parents grow up here? What stories did they tell you? How has the community changed since then?
- How is the community different today?
- What stories do you think we should preserve? Why?

Each child selected a question to ask. The students practiced reading their questions aloud to build fluency and confidence. We talked about showing respect for honored guests. We established and rehearsed interview etiquette:

- Sit straight and tall to show respect.
- Look at our guests as they speak and when you ask questions.
- Speak loudly and clearly.
- Listen with respect, interest, and gratitude.
- Ask follow-up questions; ask for stories.

The Interviews

Because of travel restrictions, it was difficult to take the students out of school, so most of the interviewees came to the classrooms. On the designated day, the honored guest was given a special chair. The children sat on the carpet. In turn, each child asked his or her question. Interviewees were impressed with the level of preparation and focus exhibited by the students. As school board member and interviewee Vince Ford said: "They asked really good questions, they were prepared and wide-eyed, and I was equally excited and wide-eyed."

The emphasis on the history and importance of community was clear in every interview. For example, Jean Hopkins talked about her position as the first Black nurse eventually becoming the assistant chief of nursing at the city's veterans' hospital and her work as an activist for the rights of African American nurses. She told the children about the city's first hospital for African Americans and about community members who went on to careers like an orchestra musician and a renowned vascular surgeon.

Ms. Myers, a longtime community resident, talked about the neighborhood's former library where she checked out books when she was a little girl and the many professions that were represented in the community. She spoke about the baseball field where families came together for barbeques but that, as a result of gentrification, was replaced by a wellness center only accessible by paying a fee. She talked about families sitting on their porches and listening to music and how, even when they had very little, her mother would send a plate of food every evening to a man who slept in the nearby park.

Mr. Ford talked about walking the same streets that the students walked. He told them that respect for elders was an important community expectation, just

Figure 5.1. Interviewing Mr. Felder at the Barbershop

as it is in the African countries. The children learned that Mr. Ford learns a new word every day; listens to blues, gospel, and R&B; and loves to travel. Mr. Ford emphasized the importance of family as an African cultural principle and that, even though his mother had passed away, he always tries to make her proud.

Mr. Felder's interview was conducted in his barbershop. Janice arranged for two 1st-graders, Javon and Anthony, to visit him. Standing respectfully with their interview questions in hand, the boys asked questions (Figure 5.1). After the interview, Mr. Felder treated them to drinks from, as they wrote, "the Pepsi machine from the old days."

Mr. Felder shared that his parents told him about their struggles and taught him to be strong. He talked about the honor of having the barbershop handed down to him 40 years earlier. He told the boys that the shop was an important place to greet old friends and make new ones. The boys giggled over Mr. Felder's use of the term *Boogie Woogie* as he shared his love of "music that is a part of our history." He told them, "The most important thing to remember is to love each other because all y'all are brothers and sisters." He shared his respect for the community: "I'm proud of this area," he said. "I went off to school, but I came back and I've been on this corner for 40 years."

Figure 5.2. Students' Notes Taken While Watching Video-Recordings of the Interviews

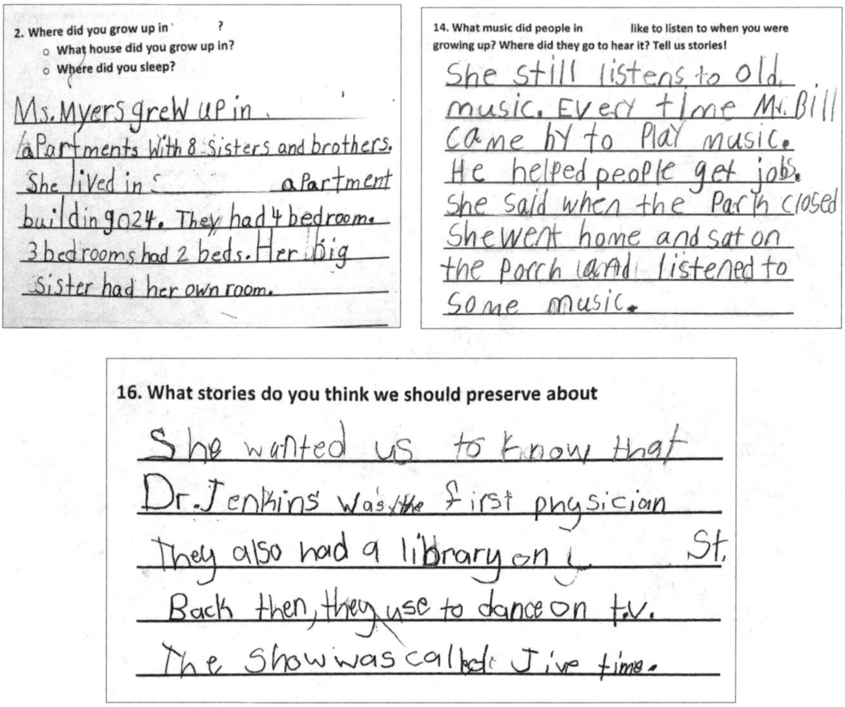

2. Where did you grow up in ?
o What house did you grow up in?
o Where did you sleep?

Ms. Myers grew up in apartments with 8 sisters and brothers. She lived in apartment building 024. They had 4 bedrooms. 3 bedrooms had 2 beds. Her big sister had her own room.

14. What music did people in like to listen to when you were growing up? Where did they go to hear it? Tell us stories!

She still listens to old music. Every time Mr. Bill came by to play music. He helped people get jobs. She said when the Park closed she went home and sat on the porch and listened to some music.

16. What stories do you think we should preserve about

She wanted us to know that Dr. Jenkins was the first physician. They also had a library on St. Back then, they use to dance on tv. The show was called Jive time.

TURNING ORAL HISTORIES INTO WRITTEN HISTORY

In the days after each interview, the children began crafting a book about the interviewee by watching the video-recording of the interview. Janice and Carmen paused the video frequently to teach note-taking skills as the students jotted down stories and quotes to use in their writing (Figure 5.2).

As the students developed their writing about the questions they had asked, Janice and Carmen taught minilessons about writing complete sentences, incorporating details and expressive vocabulary, paragraphing, and punctuating dialogue. To support students' growing knowledge about nonfiction texts, they included text features such as tables of contents and glossaries. In this way, the *Preserving Our Community Stories* series grew one book at a time (see sample pages from Ms. Myers's book in Figure 5.3). Copies of the books were presented to each interviewee.

Figure 5.3. Excerpts from Ms. Myers's Book in the *Preserving Our Community Stories* Series

---

Meet Ms. Myers

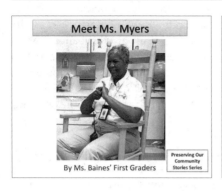

By Ms. Baines' First Graders

Preserving Our Community Stories Series

Ms. Myers grew up in our community. Her family was one of the first families to move in there. She loved living there. She said, "We had so much fun, back in the day."

Ms. Myers said that she still listens to the old music. She listened to jazz and gospel music. Every time Mr. Bill came by, he played music. He also helped people get jobs. She said that when the parked closed for the day, she used to go home and sit on the porch and listen to some music.

Ms. Myers said that the parents worked hard, they struggled for us to have something better for ourselves, for our children.

She said, "I will always remember those times. Back then, we didn't have nothing, so whatever we had was always good times."

Ms. Myers said that people had all kinds of jobs in our community. They were doctors and lawyers. Ms. Myers said that her dad was a gas station attendant. Ms. Myers' dad worked on cars and he worked on tires. Ms. Myers said that her dad did a good job on cars.

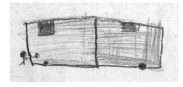

She said that the library that used to be in our community is gone. They used to go to the library and get books every week. There used to be a park by her house. They used to play there all the time. Now it is gone.

IMPACT: "THE CHILDREN ARE ME"

The reactions of students, families, and interviewees illuminated the impact of curriculum centered on respect for elders, community, and heritage. Marcus, the child described in Chapter 4 who lacked confidence in his own brilliance, made a personal connection with Mr. Ford because they had both lived in a town about 60 miles away. That connection drew Marcus into the experience. He listened intently, asked questions enthusiastically, and worked diligently on his page of writing.

Seeing himself in the children, Mr. Ford expressed gratitude for the opportunity to share his history with them:

> I have been invited to speak and asked questions but this—getting students to research my life and ask questions specifically about me, children who are taking the steps that I took, sitting in the classrooms that I sat in—this was so important to me because I wanted them to know that it was [this school] and its teachers who really inspired me. I wanted to give back some of the inspiration that was given to me. The children are me.

Ms. Williams described the impact of the barbershop interview on her son Javon's view of learning history:

> It changed [my son] in a lot of ways because he came home and was like, "Mom, I met the man at the barbershop and it was founded 75 years ago. His name is Mr. Felder!" He said, "I can learn history by going to visit barbershops."

When Mr. Felder talked about the interview, he paid tribute to Anthony and Javon and talked about Janice's commitment to creating the opportunity for children to learn from elders:

> Ms. Baines, I thought about how you were able to put the book together about my ideas and my background, how you brought the children down here, how mannerable they were, and had so much respect in my shop that day. Even the customers were impressed with how the children interacted. It tells me that you prepare them to be respectful. I'm 75 and I remember the old folks use to say, "Boy, don't you embarrass me." And that's how you were. I was glad to be able to respond. It was a great experience for me also.

Many of the children knew and adored Ms. Bonnie because she had been their kindergarten teacher. Ms. Bonnie came back for the interview after having recently retired. She summed up why the interview meant so much to her:

> We are let down so much. We are told that we can't do certain things. This made me feel like they had me on a pedestal. It made me feel that I touched

somebody's life by them wanting to be like me or by just [telling them], "Don't down yourself when you can't see your way."

By the time the books were completed, the children had learned a great deal about history and heritage. They were better able to resist and provide counterstories to damage-based narratives (Baldridge, 2017) about their community. They had grown in their respect for community elders and recognized their ability to document and preserve histories.

Although the vocabulary in the books the students created was far more challenging than the words in their instructional texts, the children persevered in reading them. Relevant content and the students' involvement as interviewers motivated them to tackle the more difficult text. The children felt their own proficiency as they wrote and read texts that mattered *to them*. And again, throughout the experience, Janice and Carmen easily addressed a range of social studies and English language arts standards.

CONTINUING TO GROW

There are many ways we could expand this work. Deepening students' critical consciousness and historical knowledge, they could do the following:

- Study oral storytelling traditions of Africa and link them to the collection of oral histories.
- Research gentrification: reasons for it, outcomes, and alternatives to it.
- Research the history of their communities from Native American origins, colonization, and enslavement through Reconstruction and Jim Crow to today; document changes over time and why they occurred.
- Compare and contrast media representations of different communities within their city; compare those representations with descriptions by community elders.
- Write counternarratives to dominant descriptions of low income communities of people of immigrants and/or African Americans; send them to newspapers, historical societies, websites, and television stations.
- Create an exhibition of students' counternarratives to honor community elders; create displays for local museums, places of worship, local universities, public libraries, and websites.

"I AM BECAUSE WE ARE"

Through this oral history project, students learned how to "conduct research by, with, and for the community" (Van Wyk & Higgs, 2012, p. 183). In the process, they grew as producers and critical consumers of literacy. As pointed out in

Chapter 1, these kinds of experiences matter for all students. Without opportunities to research and create counternarratives about communities that are typically portrayed with negativity, students will continue to internalize and perpetuate dominant narratives and stereotypes that masquerade as truths. Collecting oral histories is one way that students can counter biased, inaccurate, and/or incomplete community portraits and make a difference in their own and others' perceptions.

The children in Janice and Carmen's classrooms developed intergenerational bonds with community elders. In the process, they brought African cultural principles and practices to life—valuing elders, communal caring, and oral storytelling. The students were one step closer to understanding the Ubuntu principle "A person is a person through other persons . . . I am because we are" (Tutu, 2011, pp. 21, 22).

CHAPTER 6

Re-Membering History
Links to Africa and Literacy

> We take it back to the Motherland because I would be doing students an injustice if I did not focus on the fact that African Americans come from a history that didn't begin with slavery. Bringing Africa into my classroom makes a difference in how every child will feel the significance of Africans and African Americans in the world. —Carmen

As our work together continued, the three of us, along with Valerie Collins and Stephanie Johnson, colleagues in our original Teaching for Excellence and Equity (TEE) study group, deepened our understandings about the impact of African history on the world's knowledge. Recognizing Africa as home of the world's oldest civilizations (Wayman, 2011), we knew that an expansive and Afrocentric understanding of African history would be foundational to our curriculum, *no matter where we taught or the demographics of our classrooms*. In this chapter, we share details about our learning journey to provide examples for ways that all teachers might invest in unlearning and re-membering history (Dillard, 2012; King & Swartz, 2016) and use that learning to inform practice.

INITIATING OUR LEARNING AS TEACHERS

Our TEE group started learning about connections between West Africa and the United States by watching the film *Family Across the Sea* (Carrier, 1990). The documentary chronicles the 1989 homecoming trip taken to Sierra Leone by African American delegates from South Carolina and Georgia. The purpose of the trip was to learn, firsthand, about influences of West African culture and language on our lives in the United States, recognizing that a majority of West African people enslaved in the United States were brought through the port of Charleston, South Carolina (Burton & Cross, 2014).

This led to our visit to the Penn Center on St. Helena Island, South Carolina, one of the most important Gullah heritage sites in the country. Gullah people are descendants of West Africans who were enslaved in the low country and sea islands of Georgia and South Carolina (Campbell, 2008). The Penn Center was also the site of the Penn School, the first U.S. school for freed Africans, in operation from

1862 to 1948. The Penn Center also served a retreat for Dr. Martin Luther King, Jr., and the Southern Christian Leadership Conference, among other civil rights groups. At the Penn Center, we learned from a range of Gullah scholars, including Mr. Emory Campbell (2008), director emeritus of the center, who shared his experiences as leader of the 1989 delegation to Sierra Leone and his efforts to preserve Gullah heritage and land from resort development.

RE-MEMBERING IN SIERRA LEONE

Several years later, we had the opportunity to visit Sierra Leone ourselves. Dr. Gloria Boutte and Susi received a Fulbright-Hays Group Projects Abroad grant that funded the month-long experience in Sierra Leone for 13 educators. The goals of the trip were to re-member—to deepen our learning about historic, sociopolitical, economic, linguistic, geographic, and artistic connections between Sierra Leone and the United States and turn that knowledge into classroom practice. Our TEE group members were all participants in the trip.

The Fulbright project was called *Sankofa: Understanding Sierra Leone's History, Language, and Culture to Teach Future Generations*. The African concept of Sankofa was invoked by Dr. Boutte as a metaphor for the work we would do. The philosophy is based on the story of the mythical Sankofa bird as explained by the Akan people from Ghana and Côte d'Ivoire: Its head looks back while its body faces forward, reminding us to keep "knowledge of history in the forefront of consciousness" (Boutte, 2016, p. 65). This perfectly described our goal to re-member, retrieve, and re-center histories long denied in U.S. curriculum.

Strategies to Support Professional Study

We prepared for the trip by engaging in a range of re-membering practices that can be used by any group of teachers whether preparing to travel or learning in your own schools and communities. For example, the study group structure that grounded our learning, supported by well-chosen texts, can provide important spaces to read, talk, reflect, and plan with colleagues. Our study group was facilitated by Dr. Boutte. Her book *Educating African American Students: And How Are the Children?* (2016) details much of the information she brought to us: histories of cultural invasion and colonization, the role of pedagogy to emancipate, and structures and histories of African American Language.

Within the study group context, strategies that supported our learning in addition to reading and discussing professional literature were: viewing films, group members presenting their research into various aspects of the Sierra Leone–United States histories (economics, politics, government, geography, and educational systems), and inviting speakers from a local university. Historian Dr. Daniel Littlefield (1991) spoke about his research focused on the history of West African rice cultivation. Linguist Dr. Tracey Weldon (2003) shared her expertise in West

African language connections to the Gullah language. We made a second trip to the Penn Center, where we learned from further experts about Sierra Leone–United States connections.

As we read, discussed, viewed, and visited, we were reminded about the importance of questioning the authenticity and accuracy of historical accounts. For example, if we had only read European accounts of West African rice cultivation, we would have seen it attributed to the expertise of Portuguese explorers when, in fact, Europeans learned from West Africans and took that expertise back to Europe and the Americas (Alie, 1990; Carney, 2001).

Continuing Our Learning in Sierra Leone

Arriving in Freetown, Sierra Leone, we were met by our host, Mr. Amadu Massally. We felt a strong sense of pedagogical obligation knowing that this trip was, as Carmen said, "for our students and for ourselves, too." Janice described the trip and the learning as a gift:

> I have always known that my history was more than just slavery and I want that for my students, too. To be able to just touch the true soil of where I was from, where we all are from, was a gift. [My family sent] their girl, their gift to the Motherland. I represented the now and they wanted me to get the past.

Within a day of arrival, we began language and history studies with Sierra Leonean professors from Fourah Bay College. We continued to grow through lectures, visits to historical sites, and spending time in local schools. During the school visits, we learned more about the educational system and the ongoing stronghold of colonized thinking. Even though Sierra Leone had gained independence from England in 1961, school systems still followed British structures, and schoolbooks and posters on school walls depicted White British children. Comparisons to the United States were not difficult to make as we considered limited curricular presence of African and Indigenous traditions and languages and the lingering effects of European dominance in our own schools.

USING OUR RE-MEMBERING TO TEACH

As I began to plan for teaching about Sierra Leone, I thought about how our society would have been different if we and everyone else had been connected to our history. I could not change what had been, but I could change what I would do with my own students. —Janice

Certainly, committing to re-member and recenter marginalized, omitted, and misrpresented histories does not require a trip to Africa. While enhanced by our travel, any teacher can commit to similar learning with the benefit of libraries, the internet, local university scholars, and African and other Indigenous community members who grace almost every city in the United States. In fact, after 4 months of study in the United States and 1 month in Sierra Leone, our group had only glimpsed its history. We knew that ongoing learning was an important commitment. This also meant that, as we began to plan curriculum, if were not careful, our partial knowledge could communicate partial truths and perpetuate the very stereotypes we were trying to counter. We wanted to teach so that students would *challenge* stereotypes of Africa as defined by dark continent single stories (Adichie, 2009). We wanted students to know that from the earliest times, "languages, crops, political, and cultural influences spread outward from Africa" (Guisepi, 2001). Juxtaposed against the glaring void of this information in U.S. curricula, we were eager to bring new understandings into our classrooms.

Creating an Afrocentric Welcome to the New School Year

That August, we worked to create Sierra Leone areas in Janice and Carmen's classrooms to welcome the children on the first day of school. The areas housed Sierra Leonean drums and other musical instruments, maps, photos, posters, and brochures. Fabric from the Freetown market was draped across shelves filled with books about Africa (see text box for suggested books). We were careful to choose books that did not stereotype Africa as only about thatched huts, villages, and animal safaris. The collection included books about Africa prior to colonization, but also books about contemporary Africa selected to illustrate economic, architectural, cultural, linguistic, and geographic diversity. On the wall, maps of the world identified the continent of Africa and the country of Sierra Leone. We were careful to use maps that did not center or disproportionately enlarge Europe and North America or diminish the size of Africa.

Carmen created a wall-length bulletin board at the front of the room with the words *Links to Lineage: Literacy Through History*. This was a space for posting children's writing as they learned about Sierra Leone. Carmen presented each child with a bracelet purchased in Freetown. She told them that it represented links to Africa and they were going to learn about how all of our lives are linked to African history.

Assumptions Charts, Maps, and Virtual Travel

Carmen and Janice initiated class inquiries about Africa by creating assumptions charts. They asked the children what they knew about the continent. The students' responses were primarily stereotypical and one-dimensional: giraffes, hippos, monkeys, and lions. One child mentioned that President Obama's father was from Africa, another said that African people braided their hair, and several mentioned that Africa made them think of the ocean and beaches, but there was no knowledge of specific countries or African advancements that influence the rest of the world.

CHILDREN'S BOOKS ABOUT AFRICA

Ahiagble, G. Y., & Meyer, L. (1998). *Master Weaver from Ghana*
Branch, M. M. (1995). *The Water Brought Us*
Cohen, R. Z. (2014). *The Asante Kingdom*
Feelings, M. (1992). *Jambo Means Hello: Swahili Alphabet Book*
Feelings, M. (1992). *Moja Means One*
Kamkwamba, W. & Mealer, B. (2010). *The Boy Who Harnessed the Wind*
Knight, M. B. (2002). *Africa Is Not a Country*
McKissack, P. (1995). *The Royal Kingdoms of Ghana, Mali, and Songhay*
McNamara, C. & Provencal, C. (2010). *Nii Kwei's Day: From Dawn to Dusk in a Ghanaian City*
Medearis, A. S. (2002). *Our People*
Najjumba, J. (2014). *My First Trip to Africa*
Onyefulu, I. (1997). *A Is for Africa*
Onyefulu, I. (2015). *Grandma Comes to Stay*
Onyefulu I. (2009). *Deron Goes to Nursery School*
Raven, M. T. (2007). *Circle Unbroken*

Janice knew it was important to move her 1st-graders beyond their limited perceptions. She also wanted them to gain understandings about distances and locations, and the concept of continents versus countries. She started by bringing out a globe. The 1st-graders were able to show her the United States and even the state where they lived, but when she asked about Africa, as Janice said, "They didn't have a clue." She pointed to Africa and asked, "Is it close to us or far away? Why do you think so? How can we find out? Let's compare distances between our city and Freetown, Sierra Leone, and other distances you know."

Janice talked about the flight she had taken to Sierra Leone as she pointed to the United States and "flew" her finger across the Atlantic Ocean to Europe and then to West Africa. The next day, she decided to use a flat map. Engaging mathematical as well as geographical thinking, the larger scale on the map allowed students to focus with greater clarity on Africa in relation to North America, and to Sierra Leone as one of many countries on the continent of Africa.

Janice told the students that they were going to take a virtual trip to Sierra Leone. Addressing multiple social studies standards, they investigated the best way to travel (modes of transportation), what they needed to pack (climate), and food they would eat (regions and traditions). In Carmen's classroom, the children prepared for a similar trip by creating passports as an essential item for their journey. They discussed why passports are necessary, where they are obtained, and what they represent.

Figure 6.1. Pages from *From Africa to the Low Country to You*

Look at the three languages.
What do you notice?
What is the same?
What is different?

Wetin na yu nem? (Krio)
Wha una name? (Gullah)
What is your name? (English)

Wow, Krio and Gullah and English are
a lot a like!

Let's try a little conversation in
Krio!!

Wetin na yu nem?
Mi nem na _____.

That means:
What is your name?
My name is _____.

How are you?
Aw di bodi?

I'm fine, thank you.
Di bodi fayn.

What are you doing?
Wetin yu de du?

Good bye (I go).
A de go.

I am going home.
A de go na os.

I'll be back!
A de kam.

From Africa to the Low Country to You

To dispel stereotypes and help students see connections between life in Sierra Leone and in the United States, Carmen and Susi created a series of books with the children. One book focused on homes, clothing, and food. They intentionally included a balance of housing types found in Sierra Leone—multistory apartment buildings, small bungalows, thatched-roof homes, and mansions—to counter the children's belief that most Africans live in thatched huts. In the book, children from the U.S. and Sierra Leone were pictured in jeans and T-shirts and school uniforms, as well as historical/heritage clothing. They were depicted riding bicycles, going to school, jumping rope, and playing handclap rhymes. The books showed people in Sierra Leone carrying goods on their heads, but equally represented were people transporting goods in trucks, cars, boats, and buses. A book about languages focused on similarities and differences between the Krio language of Sierra Leone, Gullah from South Carolina and Georgia, and English (Figure 6.1).

These books became the *From Africa to the Low Country to You* series. In the process of making and reading the books, the children learned literacy as well as history, geography, and language. Carmen easily addressed multiple standards, including the differences between continents, countries, and regions; map-reading;

and understanding how cultural traditions are learned generationally and transmitted from country to country.

Dual-Language Text

Concerned that children's home and heritage languages are typically silenced by English-only ideologies, Janice and Susi also created a text to teach about and honor languages in the United States and in Sierra Leone. When they were in Sierra Leone, Susi interviewed 6-year-olds during several visits to a public school. With the teacher's help, she asked their names and what they liked to do. Returning to the United States, Susi asked the same questions of Janice's 1st-graders. From the interviews, they created a dual-language book in Krio and English. The opening pages identified a range of languages spoken in both countries, sending messages about the brilliance of multilingualism (Figure 6.2, p. 96).

The remaining pages alternated back and forth between highlighting a child from Sierra Leone and a child from Janice's class. The text on each page was written in both languages, privileging Krio by printing each sentence first in Krio with the English translation printed below:

> *Kushe-o. Mi nem na Fatmata.*
> Hello. My name is Fatmata.
> *A kmɔt Salone.*
> I come from Sierra Leone.
> *Mi gladi fɔmit yu.*
> I'm happy to meet you.
> *A lek for read buk dem.*
> I like to read books.

> *Kushe-o. Mi nem na James.*
> Hello. My name is James.
> *A kɔmɔt South Carolina.*
> I come from South Carolina.
> *Mi gladi fɔ mit yu.*
> I'm happy to meet you.
> *A lek fɔ go na store.*
> I like to go to the store.

Writing Letters

Carmen and Janice's students continued to build connections to Sierra Leone by writing letters to a class of 6-year-olds that we had visited there. The experience allowed us to push students' writing to impressive levels of detail. Their initial drafts were simplistic—"I love to play ball. What do you like to do?"—so we planned and taught minilessons focusing on including details, writing to an identified

Figure 6.2. First Pages from the Dual-Language Book Celebrating Multilingualism in Sierra Leone and in the United States

---

Mi Nem Na . . .
My Name Is . . .

A book in Krio and English
By First Grade Friends in Sierra Leone
and in South Carolina

In Sierra Leone, people speak many
wonderful languages.

Some people speak Mende.
Some people speak Temne.
Some people speak Sherbo.
Some people speak English.
Some people speak Krio.
Some people speak Limba.
Some people speak Susu.

And there are many more!!

Some people in Sierra Leone speak two or three or
four or more languages!

In the United States, people speak many
wonderful languages.

Some people speak English.
Some people speak Spanish.
Some people speak Gullah.
Some people speak Mandarin or Cantonese.
Some people speak Kikapo or Wichita or Catawba or Chickasaw.
Some people speak Hindi or Urdu or Telugu.
Some people speak Hebrew.
Some people speak Russian.

And there are many more!!

Some people in the United States speak two or three
or four or more languages!

This book is written in two
languages . . . Krio and English.

---

audience, and constructing complete sentences and paragraphs. We talked with the students about what the children in Sierra Leone might like to know about them and questions they wanted to ask their new acquaintances. We conferenced individually with students to develop subsequent drafts. With each new draft, the students' writing grew in sophistication (Figure 6.3, p. 97). The opportunity to communicate with children who lived in Sierra Leone gave purpose, authenticity, and historical connectivity to their writing.

Fables

Shortly after our trip to Africa, our Sierra Leonean host, Amadu Massally, came to the United States and visited the classrooms of teachers who had taken the trip. With him was his colleague Sulaiman Turay, who brought drums, songs, and the African art of storytelling. The children were enthralled when Mr. Turay dramatized a Sierra Leonean fable for them.

This inspired Carmen and Susi to think about how her 2nd-graders could connect Sierra Leonean fables to tales told in the United States while learning the elements of fables as required in 2nd-grade standards. They engaged the students in researching fables from Sierra Leone and Gullah fables from South Carolina and Georgia. The children created books by retelling the fables (Figure 6.4, p. 98). They also analyzed the fables for commonalities and differences, generating a list of fable characteristics. Using those characteristics, they created their own fables.

Figure 6.3. Writing Letters to Sierra Leone and Growing Through Multiple Drafts

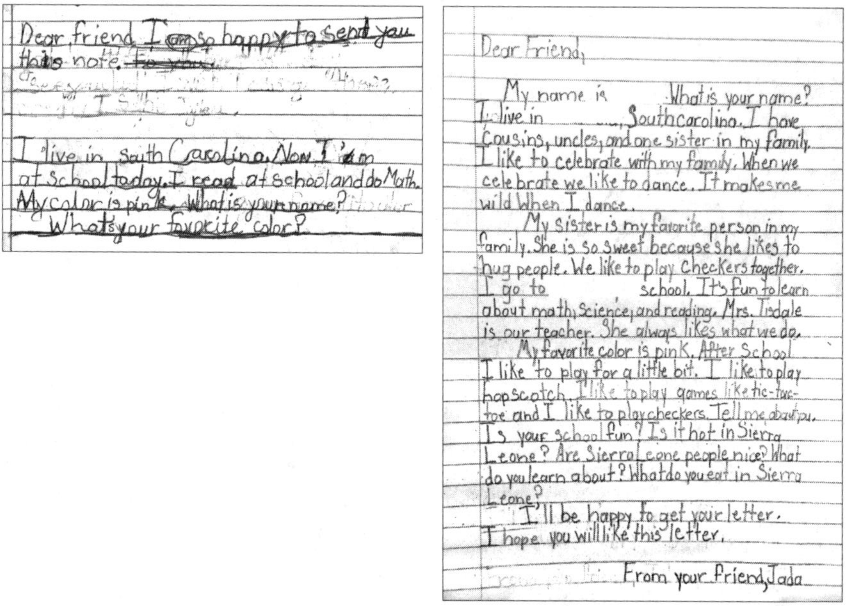

Songs

When Mr. Massally and Mr. Turay visited the schools, they taught a special song to the children—"Stop That Train." Sulaiman drew on the original Jamaican song "Spanish Town Skabeats," 1965, to write a version about traveling back to Africa, the Motherland. The rhythm and the message of the song and Sulaiman's dynamic performance drew students to it right away as we changed the language to reflect the plane flight to West Africa:

> Stop the plane,
> I want to go home.
> I want to see Africa,
> The Motherland, my home.

Janice talked with the children about the word *Motherland*, explaining why Africa is considered the "cradle of civilization." Out came the map again as Janice capitalized on the children's enthusiasm for the song by engaging her students in researching ways they could travel to the Motherland. Using their research, they wrote new verses for the song, focusing on modes of travel (a 1st-grade standard): boat, plane, submarine, and so on. Their verses were put together to make a new book, which became another addition to a classroom library.

Figure 6.4. Pages from the Children's Retelling of a Fable from Sierra Leone

Once there was a dog who was never satisfied with how much he ate. He ate and ate and ate and ate all day long!

The dog's owner – the hunter – caught a large animal for that day and he cooked it with a lot of rice. While the hunter was eating, a BIG piece of meat slipped from his fingers and fell to the ground. Do you know what that greedy dog did? He grabbed it immediately and ran away!

Looking into the water, he saw another dog looking back at him. That dog was also holding a HUGE piece of meat! The hunter's dog watched and watched. Who was this dog in the water with a gigantic piece of meat? The greedy dog wanted that meat too!

"That piece of meat looks bigger than mine," thought the greedy dog, "I want that meat!"
    Then he had a plan. "I'll bark at him and scare him away. He'll drop his meat and it will be mine!"

Interview and Biography

During Mr. Massally's visit, he introduced himself to the students as Uncle Amadu, explaining that we are all connected as family through Africa. Carmen arranged for her students to interview him. Using data from their interview, the children wrote a biography titled *Uncle Amadu: Our Family from Sierra Leone* (Figure 6.5).

This experience was instrumental in moving the children beyond their initial stereotypes of Africa. They learned that Mr. Massally's family represented a range of professions: a judge, the director of a company, a priest, a governmental leader. They learned about geographical regions (a social studies standard) as he told them about his birthplace in the town of Magburaka. Their understandings about colonization deepened when he talked about celebrating the 50th anniversary of Sierra Leone's independence from Britain. They learned about Sierra Leone's food, beautiful beaches, and its good-hearted people.

Drumming, Dancing, and History

After we returned from Sierra Leone, Janice introduced a Sierra Leonean drum to her morning gathering time. As the students gathered on the carpet, Janice played

Figure 6.5. Excerpts from *Uncle Amadu: Our Family from Sierra Leone*

Uncle Amadu:
Our Family From Sierra Leone

by
Mrs. Tisdale's
Second Grade

Table of Contents

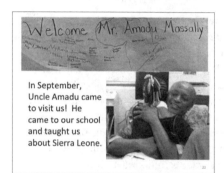

In September,
Uncle Amadu came
to visit us! He
came to our school
and taught us
about Sierra Leone.

In Uncle Amadu's family, people have many jobs.
There is a teacher and a priest. One brother is
the director of an insurance company and
another brother runs his own jeans company.

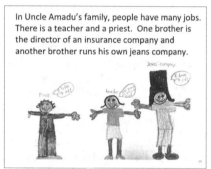

But Amadu says
that the most
precious thing
about Sierra Leone
is the people. The
people in Sierra
Leone are so nice
and friendly and
smart.

Can you find these challenging words in
Uncle Amadu's book?

continent	people	capital	education
country	arrived	taught	important
related	brought	married	featured
world	means	football	judge
activist	soccer	checkers	celebrate
accountant	uniform	international	escape
travel	college	America	independence
brilliant	famous	siblings	freedom
groups	company	insurance	season
sunshine	weather	favorite	precious

the drum and the children marked the tempo on their knees. Janice talked about how the drum was made and its uses in Sierra Leone as a form of communication and celebration. She shared videos of Sierra Leonean children and adults drumming and dancing. The children made connections to African dances that they learned in their churches or after-school programs. They began closing each day's opening by greeting one another to the beat of the drum from Sierra Leone: "Good morning, Angela. Good morning, Jalen. Good morning, Ariel. Good morning, good morning . . . Good morning, scholars."

CONTINUING TO GROW

As we think about where we could go next, a few ideas come to mind, many of which bring a critical consciousness into classroom explorations of Africa:

- Engage students in the study of how Europeans traveled to African countries centuries ago and found established governments, scientific and mathematical knowledge, art, music, and agricultural skills, in many cases advanced well beyond those in Europe; discuss why this information was/is oppressed and what students can do about it.
- Study the contributions of Africans in the United States and around the world with regard to building economic systems, roads, monuments, universities, and governmental buildings; study the conditions under which the work was done and whether or not the efforts have been attributed to Africans, supporting students in taking action (writing letters, creating video messages) if they have not.
- Study dance, drumming, and other musical arts across African countries; trace African dance characteristics to dance forms in the United States today.
- Engage students in critical analysis of texts, cartoons, websites, and films that depict Africa and Africans; to examine for misrepresentations and underrepresentation; involve them in writing letters to publishers of those texts to describe their findings and ask for change.
- Develop contacts in the cultural affairs offices of U.S. embassies in African countries to initiate long-term correspondence with children in African classrooms.
- Conduct classroom inquiries into colonization:
  » Compare and contrast histories as told by colonizers and as told by Indigenous peoples.
  » Interrogate notions like "discovery" and "civilize": What does it mean to say you discovered a land when someone else already lives there?
  » Learn about the African Diaspora. How did it come to be? What are similarities and differences across African Diasporan countries?

> » Identify Indigenous languages that were replaced with colonized languages: What happened to them? What work is being done to revitalize them? Why is that important? Create dual-language texts to contribute to language revitalization.

- Ensure that students learn something about African contributions to the world's knowledge every day: During science, introduce African scientists and inventors; during math, introduce African contributions to mathematics; during language arts, introduce authors; and so on.

"I COULD SEE THE DIFFERENCE IN HER FACE AND EYES"

The things we did in our class that really inspired me is pretty much Africa. I think teachers should bring this kind of teaching into every classroom. It would be awesome for every kid to learn about Africa. —Brion, 2nd-grader

The study of West African connections to the United States allowed us to provide purposeful literacy, social studies, science, and math instruction, but as Brion explained, heritage learning had the most enduring impact. Several years later, William, who had been a 1st grader in Janice's class, pointed out how important this kind of learning is for White students, too:

If White children don't learn about this, it would be something like racist. It would mean you don't care about Black people and Black people's history. I would feel bad because it would seem like White people are not learning anything about Black people [and] just knowing everything about White people.

Several years later, Carmen visited Jayla, a student from her 2nd-grade class who was, by then, in middle school. Jayla went to her bedroom and brought out the Sierra Leonean bracelets that Carmen had given her—her links to lineage. Jayla's mother, Ms. Woodson, talked about the impact of the experience on her daughter:

Jayla took a lot of pride from wearing those links on her arms. She loved that the most out of the whole school year. The things you taught her, I wouldn't think she would know at her age. I could see the difference in her face and eyes when she learned about Africa.

CHAPTER 7

Developing a Critical Consciousness
Silence Says, "I'm Fine with the Way Things Are"

> When people tell me that talking about issues like racism is not for little kids, my problem is that it's the reality of what's going on. They are already living it, whether they are victims of it or not. If we're not talking about it at a young age, they'll develop rose-colored glasses and pretend it's not happening or they will feel like their teachers don't care. If we settle for silence, they will not grow up able to talk about race or do anything about it. Silence is a great teacher. It says, "I'm fine with things the way they are." —Janice

Learning literacy has long been linked with addressing social justice issues in and beyond the classroom (Edelsky, 2006; Vasquez, 2014). Often called critical pedagogies or critical literacies, this kind of teaching has foundations in the work of educator-activists such as Anna Julia Cooper (1892) and Carter G. Woodson (1933), who encouraged teachers and students to reflect critically and act powerfully in and out of the classroom. This is the foundational element of culturally relevant teaching that Ladson-Billings (2017) describes as the most often neglected or misinterpreted—developing a critical consciousness. Ladson-Billings (2017) calls it the "so what?" (p. 145) of culturally relevant teaching.

There are many reasons why educators neglect, ignore, or avoid this component of culturally relevant teaching. They may not fully understand it or they are unsure of their ability to engage students in conversations about justice. Neglect also occurs when teachers assume that a critical consciousness simply means being fair and kind. Although those are certainly aspects of it, the key to critically conscious teaching means helping children identify issues of injustice, the power structures that uphold them, and strategies for taking action for change.

DAILY, DIRECT, AND FOCUSED

The incorporation of this element cannot be anything less than *daily*, direct, and focused if children are to learn how to identify inequities, develop solutions, and act on them. Examples of the normalization of criticality come from teachers such as Emily Smith-Buster (2015), recipient of the 2015 National Council of Teachers of English Donald Graves Award for Excellence in the Teaching of Writing. She creates time *every day* for specific engagements that build students' ability to speak back to injustice: literature studies that foreground authors who write about issues of justice, weekly forums on issues like atrocities in Syria and #BlackLivesMatter, students hosting a 2-day justice conference, and maintaining a justice-focused blog.

In New York City, along with a range of social justice inquiries that define her classroom, Jessica Martell's 2nd-graders problematized Columbus Day, developing understandings about colonization, power, and privilege (Souto-Manning et al., 2018). In Uniondale, Long Island, Alicia Boardman's class of predominantly Latinx immigrant 3rd-graders also discuss social justice issues daily: During the 2016 presidential election, they expressed their concerns about anti-immigrant hate speech in letters to presidential candidate Donald Trump. In Louisville, Kentucky, Shashray McCormack's (2018) elementary school students investigate the Eurocratic histories of map projections, asking questions like: Why do so many maps centralize Europe, make Africa look disproportionately smaller than it is, and position Europe and North America at the "top" and Africa and South America at the "bottom"? Also in Louisville, 1st-grade teacher Janelle Henderson and University of Louisville professor Tasha Tropp Laman worked in Janelle's classroom to engage 1st-graders in speaking back to the gentrification of their neighborhoods and deepening their knowledge about activism by interviewing members of Muhammad Ali's family (Collopy, 2016).

MAKING THE COMMITMENT

With examples like these, we know we are in good company as we join educators across the country who are committed to teaching for justice and equity. The words of Vince Ford, the school board member who was interviewed by Carmen's students (Chapter 5), provided a framework for the kind of work that needs to be done:

> We, as educators, must discuss racism candidly—both the interpersonal and the systemic. This does not mean adding a perfunctory Martin Luther King, Jr., speech to be skimmed over during Black History Month. It does not mean reading the only writer of color in the curriculum and analyzing their work, devoid of any historical context. This means holistically broadening the range of texts we expose our students to and having them interrogate why certain voices have been, and continue to be, left out of the literary and historical canons. We cannot discuss what led Dylann Roof to take the lives of nine innocent Black people with students unless we also discuss our country's history of racial violence. We cannot discuss what the confederate flag represents without also wrestling with what it means that many of our founding fathers owned slaves. These are not loosely tied phenomena; they are intrinsically linked realities and shape the country we live in.

Teaching a critical consciousness is important regardless of our pedagogical approach, but avoiding it is particularly contradictory when we pretend to be culturally relevant by accessing students' community cultural wealth (music, language, histories, heritage) without taking a stand against discrimination inflicted in those communities. In other words, when we teach through hip-hop, hand jive, and community interviews without regularly addressing issues of racial bias, we appropriate cultural wealth in disingenuous ways. As Kinloch and Dixon (2017) wrote, the home and community connections are important, but "they must be situated within an explicit engagement with teachers' anti-racist practices" (p. 332).

Janice and Carmen teach criticality in many ways. Sometimes this occurs spontaneously and other times through lessons developed specifically to address discrimination, profiling, and activism. Examples of both are shared in this chapter.

LESSONS TO BUILD A CRITICAL CONSCIOUSNESS

You aren't there for just a paycheck but you are there to try and make them better for our society. . . . You seem to be that type of person that you want all your students to be when they grow older. You want them to make our society better. —Mr. Felder, community elder

Carmen and Janice know that their students will understand more about how to address contemporary issues if they are regularly introduced to activists taking a stand. Thus, a foundation to their work to build students' critical consciousness is building classroom libraries rich in books about people standing up to injustice (see suggested titles in the following text box). We see this as an important way to create a visible focus on justice issues and sustain the study of activism throughout the year. With such texts as foundational, over the years, Carmen and Janice developed a range of lessons to help students think more about activism and their role in it.

Learning About Activism: More Than a Bus Seat

Early in their work together, Carmen and Janice were concerned that their students received only surface-level introductions to social justice activists. With this in mind, one year, Carmen decided to expand her introduction of Rosa Parks to let her students know that Ms. Parks was not a merely a tired lady who refused to give up her seat but that she was intentionally disruptive, a part of a strategically planned movement, and not the first Black woman to refuse to move to the back of the bus. Carmen also wanted her students to understand how our "racial past [connects to] ongoing racial inequities" (Brown, 2018) by introducing the civil rights movement of the 1950s and 1960s alongside the #BlackLivesMatter movement of today.

To accomplish this, Carmen wrote a story. The central character and narrator was Carmen herself as a little girl. This gave the students an immediate touchstone

---

CHILDREN'S BOOKS ABOUT ACTIVISTS

Asim, J. (2016). *Preaching to the Chickens: The Story of John Lewis*

Atkins, L. & Yogi, S. (2017). *Fred Korematsu Speaks Up*

Bollinger, M. & Tran, D. X. (2012). *101 Changemakers: Rebels and Radicals Who Changed U.S. History*

Brann, S. K. & Morales-James, C. (2017) *ABCs of Black Panther Party*

Cohn, D. (2005). *¡Sí, Se Puede!/Yes, We Can!*

Giovanni, N. (2007). *Rosa*

Krull, K. (2003). *Harvesting Hope: The Story of Cesar Chavez*

Mulholland, L. (2016). *She Stood for Freedom: The Untold Story of a Civil Rights Hero, Joan Trumpauer*

Myers, W. D. (2017). *Frederick Douglass: The Lion Who Wrote History*

Nagara, I. (2013). *A is for Activist*

Pinkney, A. D. & Pinkney, B. (2009). *Sojourner Truth's Step-Stomp Stride*

Pinkney, A. D. (2013). *Let It Shine: Stories of Black Women Freedom Fighters*

Pinkney, A. D. (2010). *Sit-in: How Four Friends Stood Up by Sitting Down*

Shabazz, I. (2014). *Malcolm Little: The Boy Who Grew Up to Become Malcolm X*

Turk, M. C. (2000). *The Civil Rights Movement for Kids*

Warren, S. E. (2012). *Dolores Huerta: A Hero to Migrant Workers*

Weatherford, C. B. (2015). *Voice of Freedom: Fannie Lou Hamer: Spirit of the Civil Rights Movement*

---

for connecting with the content. As the story opens, young Carmen is talking to her parents, who want her to go with them to a #BlackLivesMatter rally:

> Mama says those people are fighting for kids like me. They are fighting against injustice. She doesn't mean fighting with their fists, but like Martin Luther King, Jr., says, fighting with their words. Mama says words are important and powerful. . . . Who *are* these people?'

At this point, Carmen's book identifies Black leaders in the students' community: the city's first African American mayor, a member of the state legislature, a school board member, and a prominent attorney. In the book, Carmen's father explains the importance of activism, reminding her that "we stand on the shoulders of great people . . . [and these people] are making history right here in front of you." Eventually, little Carmen falls asleep under a tree and wakes up in the day of Rosa Parks. From that point, the book unveils the multilayered story of Rosa Parks that includes her work as a seamstress, participation in NAACP planning meetings, her arrest, and how it precipitated the Montgomery bus boycott.

Throughout the school year, Carmen uses the book as a jumping-off point for students' research about other civil rights leaders and discussions about current events. Conversations occur daily as the children reread the book in addition to other texts about activists. Further work building from lessons like this could include engaging students in:

- Comparing and contrasting the mission, goals, and strategies of the civil rights movement with the goals of the #BlackLivesMatter movement today
- Comparing the 1965 and 2017 marches on Washington: What was similar? Different? Who were the organizers of each march? Who participated? What did their signs say? What were their purposes? How did they organize? Who attended? What were the results?
- Creating a series of nonfiction books by researching other issues and activists with regard to Native American land rights, immigration and deportation, and contemporary and historic hate crimes against Muslims, Jews, and LGBTQIA people

Career Day: Changing the Eurocentric Narrative

Another opportunity for critically conscious teaching occurred when Carmen organized a career day for her 3rd grade. In preparation, Carmen asked her students to write about careers they saw for themselves. Initially, the responses focused primarily on sports figures and hip-hop artists. Although Carmen did not want to dissuade students from pursuing these highly skilled professions, she wanted them to see additional possibilities. Knowing that Whiteness continues to dominate most media, Carmen required her students to search websites, books, magazines, and other venues to identify people of color in a wide range of careers. Then they chose careers to research and investigated the training required, elements of the jobs, and examples of people in those positions. They created Power-Point presentations to share their knowledge.

The study of careers with an intentional focus on the underrepresentation of African Americans was important; however, the critical aspect of the lesson was guiding students to understand why a focus on African American professionals was necessary in the first place. Carmen initiated conversations asking questions such as these:

- What did you notice about the people who were depicted in magazines, on websites, and on posters and brochures? Who dominated? Who was absent? Who was marginalized?
- Why do you think this is the case?
- What can we do about it?

This is an instance when teachers can draw on their knowledge of colonization (see Chapter 2) to help students understand how we came to this place of White dominance, raising questions about how they can play a role in doing

Figure 7.1. *StarBraids and the Three Bears*

something about it. Thus, a lesson in careers can become a lesson in history and social justice by engaging students in activities such as the following:

- Tallying cultural, racial, and linguistic groups represented in particular jobs in books, media, billboards, and websites, and analyzing these for patterns of dominance, absence, and marginalization.
- Writing letters to institutions revealed in the tallies or to editors of local newspapers to share findings about (1) representation of persons of color, (2) how it impacts their views of themselves and other people, and (3) suggestions for what can be done about it.
- Inviting or arranging virtual meetings with African American, Latinx, or Native American guests from a range of professions to talk about their careers and what they see as the students' role in changing the lack of diversity across professions.

StarBraids: Powerful Black Girls

One way that Janice built her 1st-graders' critical consciousness was by emphasizing the beauty and brilliance of Black girls (Butler, 2017; Muhammad & Haddix, 2016) and instilling in them the importance of countering negative portraits (Smith, 2016). She created a book titled *StarBraids and the Three Bears*, an innovation on the story of *Goldilocks*. Janice wanted students to build literacy proficiency while creating counterstories to fairy tales that overwhelmingly define beauty and goodness as White.

Janice knew that texts reflecting the students' worlds would engage them, so she situated the story in the children's community. She used the names of streets frequented by the children so they could see an area that had been negatively profiled as a place of brilliance. The main character was StarBraids, an African American 6-year-old girl. Janice described the "beautiful designs in her braids" and illustrated the book accordingly (Figure 7.1). The focus on hair was a critical act in itself as Janice pushed back against negativity that occurs as Black children

---

Books About Children Taking Action

Gandhi, A. & Hegedus, B. (2016) *Be the Change: A Grandfather Gandhi Story*
Leitich Smith, C. & Hu, Y. (2000). *Jingle Dancer*
Levinson, C. (2017). *The Youngest Marcher*
Tafolia, C., & Teneyuca, S. (2008). *That's Not Fair! Emma Tenayuca's Struggle for Justice*
Thompson, L. A. & Qualls, S. (2015). *Emmanuel's Dream: The True Story of Emmanuel Ofosu Yeboah*
Tonatiuh, D. (2014). *Separate Is Never Equal*
Winter, J. (2014). *Malala: A Brave Girl from Pakistan/Iqbal, a Brave Boy from Pakistan*

Websites:

Embrace Race: Raising a Brave Generation. www.embracerace.org
The Conscious Kid Library. www.theconsciouskid.org

---

are sent home from school because of racist views about braided hair, dreadlocks, mohawks, or puff ponytails. Janice told the children that StarBraids had beautiful hair to reflect African traditions and a symbol of beauty.

StarBraids and her brother were proficient spellers, readers, and mathematicians: "Every day StarBraids would walk to the library and study her favorite subjects for hours." Getting lost one day after taking a new route home from the library, StarBraids ventured into a house where she found the grits "too hot" and a recliner that was "just right." When the three bears came home, they woke up StarBraids. Seeing that she had an armful of books, they asked her to read their favorite book to them, *I'm a Boundless Scholar* (Chapter 3) which she did, further proclaiming her position as a scholarly Black girl.

Reading *StarBraids* to the class was powerful in itself, but the critically conscious component came through in the students' discussion about why the book was created in the first place. Janice posed questions such as: What are differences you see between the *Goldilocks* and *StarBraids* stories? What about other fairytales you know? Why do you think that is? What can we do about it?

StarBraids also leads us to consider ways that the work can be taken further by engaging children in the following:

- Creating their own counter-fairytales, binding them as books, positioning the books prominently in the school and public libraries, and posting them on a class blog or website.
- Surveying and tallying fairytale books in the school library to identify: Which stories feature characters of color? Which feature White characters? LGBT characters? Multiple family structures? Multiple languages? What else might be missing? Why do you think that is? What can we do about it?

Figure 7.2. Excerpts from Letters to the Mayor

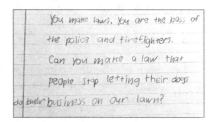

Why do we Need a traffic Light
We Need a traffic Light to help us stop if we allmost got hit Bey a car. a traffic Ligh help us to stop.

I live in the Waverly community. My neighborhood is good but we need one more stop sin on the street by Chesnut Street. A man got into a car askiden and someone almost deai. Please put a stop sin on that Street.

peoples' houses. My park is very broken. The slide is on the ground. Can you fix my park? The see saw doesn't have the thing that you sit on. Please help.

You make laws. You are the boss of the police and firefighters. Can you make a law that people stop letting their dogs do their business on our lawn?

- Investigating book recommendation websites that provide ways to evaluate children's books for authenticity, stereotype, and bias (see text boxes in Chapter 3), and engaging students in creating their own checklists to evaluate books in their classroom and school library.
- Writing letters to school and district media specialists sharing the data and recommending books.

Letters to the Mayor

Supporting her students' development of an active critical stance, one year, Carmen involved them in writing letters to the city's mayor. This occurred the year the city elected its first African American mayor. First, Carmen engaged the students in conducting research about the mayor. Social studies standards required 2nd-graders to learn about the local government. English language arts standards required reading and writing nonfiction texts. So, Carmen and the children visited the school library and filled baskets with nonfiction books about African American governmental leaders and the role of mayors. They searched for further information online. Using these materials for daily read-alouds, independent reading, and literature discussion groups, the students learned and practiced reading skills while learning about basic functions of the mayor's role and the history of Black leaders.

But Carmen wanted students to dig deeper, so she opened discussions about their right and responsibility to bring their voices to local government: What did the mayor's position mean in their own lives? How did his position affect them? What was their role in communicating concerns to him?

The students brainstormed issues in their communities. They drafted and redrafted business letters to the mayor. They wrote about positive aspects of their community like having fun with their families and friends. They also shared community concerns and asked the mayor for help (Figure 7.2). In the process, the students learned literacies while recognizing their agency, ability, and responsibility to bring issues to the attention of people in positions of power.

Continuing to build students' sense of agency from this experience, they could do the following:

- Learn further strategies for effecting change by reading about other children taking action.
- Write follow-up letters to the mayor or create video messages to find out what steps are being taken to address their concerns.
- Interview members of the community to learn about other issues of concern, and write letters to state and local legislators, editors of the local newspaper, websites, and television stations to express those concerns.
- Conduct a survey of the number of people of color in governmental positions in the city, state, country, and write letters conveying data to people who hold positions of power with regard to those offices.
- Invite local governmental leaders to talk about effective ways to impact change.

DEVELOPING A CRITICAL CONSCIOUSNESS
THROUGH SPONTANEOUS CLASSROOM TALK

We teach ABCs & 123s, but if we're not having our kids think critically about injustice, what good are you doing in the end? Andra Day's song says, "It don't mean nothing, if you don't stand for something." Our kids need to stand for something. It gives meaning to their lives. —Carmen

Although Janice and Carmen planned specific justice-focused lessons, some of the most important critical conversations occurred in unplanned moments when the children, Janice, or Carmen brought up local or national events or when issues were revealed in students' comments or actions. In these moments, Janice and Carmen never shied away from the need for critical talk. No question or issue was off-limits and every student's voice was heard.

Responding to Local Events

Having established, from the first weeks of school, that their classrooms were places where social justice talk was the norm made it possible for Janice and Carmen to respond to local and national situations as they occurred throughout the year. With this foundation, Janice was able to talk with the children following a police raid in their neighborhood. Many of her 6-year-olds came to school that day having just seen neighbors or family members taken to jail and police everywhere. On a day when the students needed to feel safe and when silence would only exacerbate their fears and confusion, the requirement to enforce paced curriculum needed to be set aside. As Janice said, the children "literally just needed to breathe," so she helped them talk through and write about their fears and frustrations:

> I had kids crying and confused, so of course I sat mine down and told them, "Don't think this was supposed to happen to you. This is not something that should automatically happen." We talked about the police taking such forceful action and options for how they could have handled it. We also talked about the arrests: "You know how sometimes you make choices to do the wrong thing? It was like that. The people who broke the law just made a bad decision, a wrong call."

Given her own critical consciousness, Janice was upset that "in the midst of this, people were still running around worrying about test data without thinking about what the children had witnessed that morning":

> I was like, "Did you add this to your data?" So I'm supposed to say, "Okay, boys and girls, let's do math." My kids need to talk and write out their feelings. They need to feel they have some control over the situation.

As Janice ditched planned curriculum to create space for talk, multiple elements of critically conscious teaching came into play: (1) Janice acted on the children's need to make sense of a frightening situation rather than focus in that moment on test preparation; (2) the children's trauma, if not addressed, could have an even more devastating effect on them emotionally, behaviorally, and academically; (3) the very act of critical reflection through opportunities to talk and write would reinforce a range of academic and sociopolitical skills; and (4) perhaps most important, taking advantage of the moment to engage in talk meant that students continued to build trust in Janice as someone who would not close down their need to explore issues of justice.

Janice's discussions further developed a classroom culture that said, "This kind of talk is welcomed here." As a result, when other issues came up, the space was already created for discussion: "What are you hearing?" "What do you worry about?" "Why do you think this is happening?" "How can we help change things?" Janice worked every day to normalize these kinds of conversations. As she explained: "It's what you do. If you're not having those conversations regularly, that's why it's uncomfortable."

"He's So Smart!": Internalized Racism in 2nd Grade

In Carmen's classroom one year, an incident occurred that revealed how easily racism can lead to self-degradation and notions of White superiority in the minds of children. That year, all the children in Carmen's class were African American except Jason, who was European American. Within days after Jason joined the class, Carmen noticed that he was put on a pedestal by his peers as the "smart one."

Every day, Carmen engaged the class in what she called Mental Math exercises. She wrote problems on the board and the children called out answers and explained the steps they took to arrive at them. Every day, more than a few children consistently had the correct answers; however, the students always focused on Jason: "Jason's so smart!" "Let Jason answer!" They never announced their African American peers' expertise. In a strong example of internalized racism, the 3rd-graders *expected* Jason, the European American child, to know the answers, but not their African American peers. Echoing decades of research about young children and race (see Chapter 1), the students had learned a superiority of Whiteness that went hand in hand with feelings of Black self-degradation (Perry, Steele, & Hilliard, 2004).

Carmen worked through numerous conversations with the students to address this deeply ingrained bias, but it was difficult to shake. Regularly, she talked about the fact that they were *all* smart. But talk was not enough. She began writing their correct responses on the board with their names beside them. She pointed to their names to show them that their responses were exactly the same: "Look, Damien, Jamal, and Jason *all* have the same answer!" She also began paying more attention to her own responses to Jason: Did she favor him in ways she had not noticed before? Did she call on him more? Praise him more? What about her facial expressions and responses to behaviors? What might she be inadvertently communicating?

After a few weeks, the children stopped highlighting Jason, but their internalized views of White superiority had come through loudly and clearly. Looking back, we thought about how it was important not only to interrupt internalized racist notions but also to help students understand why they were thinking that way. Some pedagogical actions come to mind:

- Teach the term *internalized racism*. Share examples of how and why people start to believe or disbelieve their own brilliance because of messages they receive. Involve students in examining messages in their lives. Talk about these messages and help them take action in response.

- Normalize stories of Black genius as a part of classroom life *every day* using books, websites, and social media video clips.
- Engage students in learning how we came to be raced. Discuss how and why racism has been taught and internalized from the days of European colonizers.
- Share video clips of people speaking back to bias (there are many on social media), and engage students in creating their own.

Colorism and Hair

Another example of internalized bias was revealed one day in Carmen's class of African American kindergartners. It was in the midst of a lesson about Dr. Charles Drew, the African American physician and scientist who pioneered the desegregation of blood donorship and initiated the first blood banks. Carmen was reading aloud from a picture book about him when one of the girls pointed to his picture and called out, "Oooh, he's so shiny!"

"What do you mean?" Carmen asked.

"It's so beautiful; it's so nice," other girls called out. Carmen probed for reasons why the girls were impressed with Dr. Drew. Their responses revealed their focus on his light skin tone. Carmen knew she had to stop the lesson and change gears:

> In that moment, it was more important for them to gain a sense of pride about their skin color. They needed to be proud of themselves, and their families and friends. But I wasn't really prepared. I knew about light skin–dark skin bias but now here I was with my 5-year-olds, so I had to figure out what to say. If they had this feeling already, how could I change their perception?

Carmen's students had internalized a racial bias called colorism taught from the time of colonizers as a mechanism to gain and sustain control by creating the illusion that beauty and intelligence are connected to lighter skin. During that time, 18th-century German philosopher Christoph Meiners coined the racist term *Caucasian*, labeling people from the Caucasus region of Europe and Asia (now the countries of Georgia, Azerbaijan, and Armenia) as having the whitest, "most beautiful skin" and equating it with intelligence (Jensen, 2005). This concept also appeared in the work of anthropologists like Johann Blumenbach, who promoted bogus racial classification as intelligence markers (Painter, 2011). Colorism continues to fuel businesses that promote skin-lightening products around the world and impacts everything from hiring and admissions practices to racist profiling and violence (Monroe, 2017).

"Do you like it better than your skin?" Carmen asked the children.

"Yes."

Figure 7.3. Kindergartners' Writing

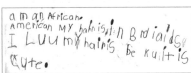

"My hair is in braids.
I love my hair because it is cute."

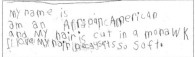

"I am African American
and my hair is cut in a mohawk.
I love my hair because it is so soft."

Carmen explained that they were all beautiful and that their ancestors gave African Americans beautiful skin in many shades. She asked if they remembered what *African American* means and they talked about beauty of Africans, later sharing photos of well-known Africans and African Americans of varying skin tones.

Carmen's class discussion did not stop with skin. She went on to discuss hairstyles and texture. The book *Hair Dance* (Johnson, 2007)—a celebration in photographs and verse of African American girls' hair—was in her classroom collection, so Ms. Delaughter, Carmen's co-teacher and kindergarten teaching assistant, read the book to the children. As she read, Ms. Delaughter talked about how her own locks were an important part of her beauty and pride as a Black woman and how her hair represented African histories of hair design and spirituality. The students wrote about what they loved about their own hair (Figure 7.3) and shared their writing with one another.

The next day, Carmen went back to the study of Charles Drew; however, having interrupted it to follow a path initiated by the students created an important opportunity to develop their critical consciousness. When families came to school for the students' presentation of Black history projects, Carmen shared the children's comments. She talked about the importance of having conversations at home so that children understand the racist histories of colorism and believe in the beauty of themselves, their peers, and their history.

From that time, Carmen has remained alert to teaching so that her African American students know and believe that "they are wonderfully made and their skin and hair are beautiful." However, she sees this as just as important when she teaches European American students—teaching the history of colorism and the beauty of Blackness:

I want my Black students to be proud of the curls in their hair and the color of their skin. But I need for my White students to get that message about Black people, too. When I have White students, I want them to see just as much beauty in their Black and Brown peers as I do.

Charleston: Coming to Students with Love and Truth

On June 19, 2015, Reverend Clementa Pinckney, Cynthia Hurd, Susie Jackson, Ethel Lance, Depayne Middleton-Doctor, Tywanza Sanders, Daniel Simmons, Sharonda Coleman-Singleton, and Myra Thompson were murdered in a brutal racist act as they worshipped in Mother Emmanuel African Methodist Episcopal Church in Charleston, South Carolina. The church was 90 miles from the school where Janice taught 5- through 10-year-old African American and European American children in a summer program. Janice's response to her students' fears and questions provides another example of addressing in-the-moment events without shying away from them.

The day after the massacre, the children came to Janice full of talk about the murders and the funeral being planned. They were forthright in their questions, revealing their fears and confusion: What had happened? How could adults allow this to happen? How can we stop it from happening again? How can we be sure that we're safe, that our friends are safe? Janice knew it was important to help them see the situation from a historical perspective. She didn't want to frighten them but she also knew the importance of not sanitizing or "shy[ing] away from harsh and difficult realities" (Haddix & Sealey-Ruiz, 2016, para. 3) and that a sense of helplessness would only breed further fear and despair:

> I needed to make them feel safe, but it was also important to help them see history and how it had repeated itself. They had to have some idea of the horrors caused by racism. I want them to grow into adults who would never inflict such atrocities. They had to think about how this could stop. To do this, I knew I had to come to every child with love, but also truth.

While showing them her love and protection, Janice wanted the students to know that this was not an anomaly, that African Americans had been historically targeted in places of worship. Janice felt that knowing history along with current events was critical to helping the children understand the ongoing need for change and the role they could play in it. So, she started by explaining:

> Have you ever heard the story about the four little girls who were killed in a church in Alabama? This was 60 years ago. They were killed in their church basement when someone planted a bomb and blew up the church.

Janice found a video clip about the Birmingham bombing on her iPad. The children watched as family and church members spoke about their devastation and grief. They looked at photographs of Addie Mae Collins, Carol McNair, Carole Robertson, and Cynthia Wesley and saw that they were friends. They saw Black and White people crying. They saw the remnants of the church, the glass. As they viewed the videos, the children were very quiet. Then Janice said to them, "That's one reason why today everyone is upset. We are very sad for the people who died and we are also sad because this is something that's already happened and shouldn't have happened again."

Janice knew that the children needed to understand the event as a part of a broader history of violence against Black people and that the only solace to be found was by offering comfort and empowering students to act for change. She continued, "Let's think about what we can all do so it doesn't keep happening."

Responsibility, Not Guilt

A challenge that Carmen and Janice often discussed was how to engage students in conversations about discrimination, profiling, and privilege without generating hate for people who look like those perpetrating atrocities or invoking guilt in White children for the deeds of their ancestors or contemporaries. Carmen wanted to be sure that, instead of guilt, discussions of racism led students to take responsibility for taking action against racism:

> I didn't want my White kids to feel guilty. Seeing someone who looks like them treating someone badly who looks like me could be traumatizing. However, I do want them to know that we all have a responsibility to do something about it. I make sure they know that I love them and that it's up to all of us to work to change injustices. I don't make excuses for what their ancestors did or what White people do today, but I do want to show them how they can be change-makers.

This led Carmen and Janice to be even more intentional in finding out exactly how the students interpreted class discussions. Janice explained:

> You really have to listen to find out what they are thinking, what impressions they are getting or you don't know what message you're sending. That's why conversation is so important. You don't know what kids know if you're not talking to them. You don't know where their thinking may go astray or where they just fell off and stopped listening.

Every classroom example presented in this chapter provided an opportunity for Janice and Carmen to listen to children and correct misperceptions. However, the move from talk toward action was key to putting guilt aside and finding the courage and confidence to move forward in productive ways.

"WHY IS IT NOT LIKE BREATHING?"

You want to know why we should teach a critical consciousness? I ask why it is not as much of a necessity as teaching the alphabet. Why it is not like breathing? Why would you not do this? —Janice

The alternative to nurturing abilities to identify and speak back to injustices is educational silence. This indicates to students that we do not care enough to try to change systems that marginalize them and people around them. When people question the necessity of developing a critically conscious classroom, Janice's words help us stand behind our responsibility as professionals:

Of course we have to teach a critical consciousness. I have to be in spaces all the time where I'm already labeled because of race. My students of color experience the same thing. We can't raise any more new generations who don't know how to identify injustice and take action against it. If you have given your life to young children, then you have to have the guts to figure it out.

In teaching, above all other professions, we are positioned to "have the guts to figure it out." When we listen to our students, their families, and community members, we know that professing neutrality or invoking silence are conscious stances "that work against social justice" (Milner, 2015, p. 11), so the choice is clear. As Ernest Morrell, past president of the National Council of Teachers of English, told assembled educators in his 2015 presidential speech: "If you are not for social justice then you are for social injustice. There is no in-between."

CHAPTER 8

Culturally Relevant Teaching as the Pedagogical Norm

> Hey, Black child, I wish the world could see you for your greatness, your
> beauty, and your intelligence. Sometimes you may feel that you are the only
> one in the world who has to find your value. But I see you! And I will affirm
> you because you matter. You are essential to this class, to this school, and to
> the world. No matter who I teach, I will create experiences that allow every-
> one to see how influential your people are in the development of this country,
> this world. —Janice

Inspired by Useni Eugene Perkins's (2017) poem "Hey, Black Child!" Janice makes
a promise to the children under her care. The practices and convictions shared in
this book are inspired by our belief in that promise. It encompasses a commitment
to gain more complete and accurate understandings of African and African American contributions to the world's knowledge. It is a promise to use that learning
to evaluate curricula and materials and generate new practices that re-center and
normalize that which was stolen, marginalized, or distorted, and create a more just
curricular whole. It is a commitment to provide students with a lens to recognize
injustices and stand against them. It is a promise to interrogate discipline policies,
family–school relationships, special education and gifted-and-talented programs,
and assessment practices to identify and take action to dismantle and replace systems that privilege and oppress. *For us, this means committing to culturally relevant, humanizing, and decolonizing teaching as the pedagogical norm.*

We hope the stories and resources offered in this book provide substance
for critical reflection as we work toward this goal. This chapter supports those
reflective and transformative moves by (1) addressing dissonances and challenges
encountered in the work, and (2) offering strategies for action in support of the
move toward change.

CHALLENGES

The rewards of working to generate humanizing, decolonizing, and culturally relevant pedagogies are many: positive academic, cognitive, critical, motivational, and

psychological impact on students; teachers' reenergized excitement for teaching and feeling a sense of pedagogical ownership; being more in tune with students; and knowing that we are a part of a movement to overhaul systems that oppress and privilege. This does not mean, however, that the work is without challenges.

Standards and Autonomy

As we navigate the world of standards and pacing guides, concerns about rigid standardization and the imposition of scripted programs are real. Not the least of these concerns is that standards often represent a form of ongoing colonization requiring teachers to hold students to Eurocentric norms. However, while we work to change these norms, our students cannot wait, so we fully implement culturally relevant teaching within standards systems while simultaneously taking action for change. We do this in a variety of ways.

We don't succumb to myths. We are careful not to succumb to "they say you have to" myths that abound in schools (Long et al., 2006). We have all heard the myths: "You can't do that because of standards" or "You have to use the books on the standards list" or "You can only teach writing for 30 minutes a day." However, autonomy is often hidden in plain sight once we get beneath the mythology of "they said." For example, a common myth is that standards require the use of specific books, when in fact, most standards documents merely suggest book titles (Long, Hutchinson, & Neiderhiser, 2011). Also, standards-driven time allotments can be viewed constructively. Who says that writers workshop or independent reading can't extend into the time scheduled for social studies or science, particularly when students are writing and reading about social, historical, and scientific issues using nonfiction texts?

We start with students. Our instructional planning always starts by thinking about students, families and communities, hidden figures and histories, and the development of a critical consciousness. *Then* we look at standards, knowing that it is incredibly easy to align culturally relevant content with standards of any kind. However, what seems obvious to us is not always obvious to the administrators and colleagues who walk into our classrooms, so we are always familiar enough with standards to demonstrate how they are addressed in the work we do.

We build knowledge. We constantly build our professional knowledge and use it to assure families, administrators, and colleagues that we are teaching students according to some of the best and most current research. This includes research that illuminates reasons why many teaching approaches are *not* equitable because of a history of colonized thinking (see Chapters 1 and 2). We also call on research that documents how students read more, engage more, learn more, and attain higher grade point averages when they are taught in contexts that are meaningful to them (Dee & Penner, 2016; Long, 2004). We access work that illustrates how children in culturally relevant classrooms not only learn skills but *use* literacies, mathematics, science, and social studies to conduct research, articulate knowledge, effect change, and continue to grow (Delpit, 2012; Mahiri, 1998).

We reject and replace dehumanizing practices. When curricular topics *are* rigidly mandated, we flat out refuse to teach those that reflect racist and colonized views of history, but we make clear why we are doing so and we share alternatives. For example, if the requirement is to teach about Native Americans in November, we do not merely reject colonized texts but we also engage students in investigating how colonized narratives came to be, teaching them to seek Indigenous perspectives. Students can use that knowledge to analyze, critique, and take action against representations in textbooks, curricula, media, greeting cards, costume shops, institutional decorations, and so on. They can research, discuss, and respond to issues ranging from wearing Indian headdresses to historical and contemporary attempts to violate sacred Indigenous lands. They can take part in the work to revitalize Native American and other Indigenous languages, and highlight powerful intersections across Native American, African American, Latinx, and Asian histories.

These kinds of engagements come with an important caveat. King and Swartz (2014) warn that merely teaching colonized curriculum from a critical stance without doing the work to actually decolonize it keeps us "wedded to dominance" (p. 11). We agree. To effect and sustain change, we must also raise our voices, backed up by knowledge, as a part of the commitment to overhaul policies and practices (see strategies later in this chapter).

We just do it. Finally, we get busy and get on with it. For example, when we saw that the instructional text collection in the school's book room was dominated by Whiteness, we created books with and for the children and provided titles for the school media specialist to order. This was easy to justify when we recognized that, using culturally relevant texts, students read more and with greater enthusiasm and deeper comprehension, tackled more difficult texts, and were more likely to transfer content knowledge and literacy skills to other genres (trade books and tests) than when using packaged sets provided for literacy instruction.

All of this is to say that we do not need to be halted in the work of culturally relevant teaching because of standards and pacing guides. But we *do* have a responsibility to fight for long-term and sustainable change to normalize culturally relevant pedagogies so we do not have to be subversive to be able to teach equitably.

Testing

Testing is always a frustrating challenge, but particularly when we consider its racist origins. It is widely acknowledged that "standardized tests are narrowly normed along White, middle class, monolingual measures of achievement"

(Ladson-Billings, 2017, p. 143). We know that "modern assessments are holdovers from the early part of the 20th century when psychologists thought they could isolate the racial markers for intelligence" (Singer, 2016) and used those theories to "justify the existing racial order [with] the false promise of measuring everyone equally, accurately, and fairly" (Knoester & Au, 2014, p. 7). This became "a self-reinforcing cycle of racism" (p. 8). In fact, the Scholastic Aptitude Test (SAT) was developed in the 1920s expressly to exclude immigrants, Native Americans, and African Americans from the nation's elite (Singer, 2016).

They Know More Than Tests Show

It is easy to notice bias in today's assessments when we consider how standardized tests and many classroom-based assessments *conceal rather than reveal* what children know (Mills, 2005). For example, Carmen talked about ways students' knowledge is concealed when assessments do not recognize home languages or abilities to translate across languages:

> [In some tests] you're supposed to take off points because the child didn't say the ending of the word; however, this occurs in many languages and language variations. The thing is that the children demonstrate more cognitive ability when they read the word written on the test and then translate it to the way they say it. Not being able to value that means that the test has failed not the child. You're penalizing them for being good at translation.

In Susi's work with preservice teachers, she regularly observes the university students contrasting what they learn about children through culturally relevant practices (many of the practices described in this book) with the labels of inability imposed through conventional assessments. In Susi's literacy course, the university students work with children designated by the school as "struggling readers." However, this labeling is not revealed to the preservice teachers until the end of the semester, when they are always incredulous at the deficit stamping of children they have come to know as brilliant: "But I thought I had the smartest student in the class!"

Using culturally relevant measures, children always show that they know more than conventional measures can demonstrate. Remember Ileka, the little girl in Chapter 4 who rarely engaged with texts? No standardized test could highlight the progress she exhibited when "My Girl" captured the spirit, focus, and reading ability of a child who had been disenfranchised from reading. Or consider Jamon, the student who read far above grade level but seemed unhappy and unengaged. Jamon was not working up to his capabilities until the opportunity to conduct research prompted by the "Black History Is Our History" rap moved and motivated him. Understanding Jamon's growth in engagement, sense of purpose, and ability to conduct research could not have happened with typical standardized tests. Similarly, standardized tests would not have illuminated the children's growth in revering elders and capturing oral histories, their understanding of complex issues of colorism, the ability to use literacy to speak up about injustices, or their cognitive and social expertise in translating home literacies into conventions of schooling.

The failure of conventional assessments to capture these impressive achievements (Basterra, Trumbull, & Solano-Flores, 2011) and the consequent labeling of students constitutes racial, ethnic, and linguistic profiling that needs to be protested at every level of our educational system. However, while we work to challenge and replace unjust systems of assessment, we will continue to lose children to labeling and subsequent loss of self-esteem and opportunity if we don't provide access to success as measured conventionally. Janice explains that it's up to teachers to recognize this and respond:

> There are people in this world who don't want [our students] to be successful because of their race or who try to reject them and have low expectations because of their socioeconomic status. There are so many different forces around them that will not try to make room for them, so it's up to us to help them create their own space with the knowledge we're providing them. Testing is one of those spaces.

Strategies for Raising Testing Consciousness

Janice and Carmen begin building students' testing savvy by introducing hidden secrets of testing and then supporting students in using their culturally relevant knowledge to outwit the culturally irrelevant testing game. Janice begins by explaining testing realities to them:

> When you take a test, you have to think—the people who made that test don't know you like I know you. I know how smart you are. But this test is the only way they are going to try to figure you out. So, you have to outsmart them.

Show what you know. One strategy Janice uses is asking students to "show what you know" when people come to visit the classroom. She tells the children that this is much like showing their knowledge on tests: "People who visit our classroom are like people who make the tests. They don't know you, so you have to show them what you know." In this way, Janice helps students build confidence as they show their knowledge for guests.

Name what you know. Carmen teaches students to name what they know using terminology that they will find on tests. For example, when they were writing Amadu Massally's biography (Chapter 6), she guided students to name tested nonfiction features as they created them: "What do you call the page with all of the chapter titles and page numbers? How can our Table of Contents help us find a story about jobs in Sierra Leone?" Then she teaches the children to transfer that knowledge to Tables of Contents in trade books and is explicit in telling them that they will be asked to identify Tables of Contents on tests.

Practicing test formats using culturally relevant texts. One year, Carmen and Susi used the class-made book *Music We Love!* (Chapter 4) to plan support for a specific kind of test-taking savvy. At that time, the district evaluated children's writing and spelling using dictation exercises from a prepackaged kit. Carmen knew that lack of familiarity with the assessment format would make it difficult for students to show their knowledge. To build familiarity, she engaged them in daily 5-minute dictation exercises using sentences from a book they knew well, *Music We Love!* She gave instructions using scripted language from the assessment guide, inserting familiar language from *Music We Love!*:

> I am going to read the beginning of a story. I will read it once all the way through, then I will begin at the beginning again and read each word one at a time. Listen carefully and write what you hear or expect to see for each word in the sentences: *My name is Carmen. I love "My Girl." I love it because it makes me happy.*

In the process of gaining comfort with the language of the assessment and the dictation format, Carmen taught the students to use their culturally relevant knowledge in the testing context:

> You know how to write the word *name* from our book. So, if you know how to write *name*, how do you think you would spell *game*? When you take the test, remember that you know how to write a lot of words; try to see those words in your mind and then write them.

Time and Energy

Sometimes teachers express the concern that culturally relevant teaching is time-consuming. Yes, it takes more time than parroting a script or copying lesson plans from the Internet. However, no publisher of scripted programs can possibly know our students, the local community, critical issues of the day, or our teaching styles. Most important, although websites like Teaching Tolerance (www.teachingtolerance.org), Teaching for Change (www.teachingforchange.org), and Rethinking Schools (www.rethinkingschools.org) offer excellent advice for critically conscious teaching, many other websites offer lesson plans under the guise of culturally relevant teaching that reify the stereotypes, cultural simplifications, and colonized approaches we seek to change.

So, how do we make time to invest in the work? First, we see this kind of teaching as connected across the day. This allows us to go deeply, rather than jump from one lesson to another. As Carmen said, "Before this, my teaching felt scattered and rushed most of the time. Now I feel more focused. I see the day connected in ways I didn't before."

Second, we use time differently. We replace wastes of time with effective uses of time. No more grading worksheets at night. Instead, we assess and provide feedback *while we teach*, knowing that our preparation time at home is better spent building our own knowledge rather than scrawling checkmarks and smiley faces on worksheets that do nothing to further children's growth. Sitting side by side in regular student conferences and paying attention and responding to students during large- and small-group work are much more effective ways to assess and provide feedback.

Managing time and energy can also be addressed by enlisting students and family members. For example, we can do much of the research to relearn histories *with* students and families as we uncover hidden histories together.

We do, of course, get tired, but we are also fired up and energized. We find tremendous joy knowing that we can play a role in shaping a more just society because our pedagogical choices will find their way into children's consciousness, anchoring their developing views of the world, themselves, and one another.

STRATEGIES FOR ACTION

We have written about teaching in culturally relevant ways within and beyond existing systems, but also about the need to transform the larger institutions in which we work. The fact is that when we do not engage in changing the bigger picture, we perpetuate the very systems we hope to overhaul. Asante (2017) provides a vivid metaphor for this tendency: "One cannot simply add Latino, African, Native American, and Asian information into the white bottle and shake it up and get what is necessary for all students. *The bottle must be changed* [emphasis added] . . . all else is nothing but domination" (p. 27).

To support educators' creation of a new bottle, we offer suggestions for reflection and planning for change to be used in conjunction with the reflective questions and resources in Chapter 2. We hope these recommendations will be helpful for long-term professional learning in faculty study groups, home–community–school planning, districtwide work, individual teacher reflection, and preservice/inservice teacher education:

1. **Do your homework:** You will be better able to articulate why this kind of teaching is important for children and for humanity when you are knowledgeable. See the professional book lists in Chapter 2 and this book's Reference list for resources to support ongoing study.

2. **Reflect together:** Use professional reading to think together about and define terms and concepts such as *colonization, privilege, oppression,*

marginalization, distortion, humanization, dehumanization, stereotype, Eurocractic, decolonization, re-center, normalize, and *sustain.*

3. **Take a reflective walk:** Walk through your school with these concepts in mind. Pay attention to the walls, texts of all kinds, computer applications, curriculum, assessments, academic and discipline referrals, and testing practices as you walk through the front doors, into the front office and the teachers' lounge, down the halls, and into the library, art, and music rooms. Stop by an IEP or RTI meeting and then go into your own classroom. Ask:

   - Who dominates and is thereby humanized, normalized?
   - Who is dehumanized through omission, marginalization, misrepresentation, and stereotype?

4. **Look for criticality:** Do you see evidence of students and teachers regularly engaged in identifying and taking action against injustices (beyond canned-good drives) as a curricular norm?

5. **Look at your teaching:** Does your classroom and your curriculum provide opportunities for students to blend home, community, and school knowledge? Does your teaching normalize literacies from home, community, popular culture, and a range of languages? How do you ensure that each student's brilliance is visible to every other student? Do you ensure that marginalized histories, literature, sciences, art, and contributors to the world's knowledge are normalized by teaching about them every day?

6. **Reflect through students' and families' eyes:** As students and families walk through your school and into your classroom, what might they think about who matters more and who matters less to educators in these spaces?

7. **Plan for change:** Based on these reflections, what changes do you need to make as a teacher, school, grade level? How will you bring silenced or marginalized histories, hidden figures, communities, languages, literacies, and critical issues to life as *normalized* even when you and your students do not represent silenced groups?

8. **Build a critical foundation:** How will you incorporate a foundation of justice as a daily norm? How will you connect—locally and virtually—with networks of other teachers engaged in social justice teaching?

9. **Connect with and learn from families:** How will you ensure that you learn regularly from and with families in ways that *they* see as safe, productive, and respectful of their knowledge? How can you use that knowledge to generate new policies and practices that center families' wisdom?

10. **Learn more about testing:** How do current assessment systems sustain socioeconomic and racial hierarchies? Learn from others who have taken a stand against unjust testing; stand with them.

11. **Document your work:** Make your culturally relevant teaching visible by collecting evidence about its impact on students' motivation and growth: Take digital photos of student work, interview students and families about your teaching, and document conventional as well as culturally relevant assessment results.

12. **Speak up:** Use your documentation to share insights in faculty meetings; at district, state, and national levels; and with local media. Engage students and families in presenting with you. Develop a task force to examine policies and practices and plan for change.

13. **Learn and take a stand for a lifetime:** Make a plan and commitment for keeping your own critical lens sharp and holding yourself accountable for ongoing professional learning. Take a stand for justice in and out of school. Carry out the plan.

"NO MORE COMFORTABLE SILENCE"

In the summer of 2015, President Barack Obama spoke at the funeral of Reverend Clementa Pinckney who, along with eight of his beloved parishioners, was murdered in Mother Emmanuel Church in Charleston, South Carolina. Many of the President's words stay with us, but one sentence speaks particularly to teachers' work for justice. He said, "It would be a betrayal of everything Reverend Pinckney stood for . . . if we allowed ourselves to slip into a comfortable silence again" (Obama, 2015, para. 36).

When something as horrific as the murder of nine people occurs, much attention is given. Soon, however, a silence descends, a silence that is only comfortable for those protected by it. As we consider our role in changing an unjust status quo in schools, we know that every student also suffers when we are silent with regard to issues of equity. We know that change is necessary.

For the field of education, change will require "a paradigm shift from a culture of denial" (Regan, 2010, p. 189) to one in which we are comfortable questioning "what constitutes normalcy and how teachers implicitly and explicitly reproduce it" (Matias & Liou, 2015, p. 610). Then we must transform policy and practice accordingly. We see these as first steps toward "teaching for freedom" (King & Swartz, 2016, p. 21). We invite you to join us in taking these steps by standing for what Nathaniel Bryan calls "not-on-my-watch pedagogy—bold and unapologetic ways of saying, 'Not today or any other day will I stand by while injustices in classrooms or society continue'" (personal communication, September 10, 2017).

In that spirit, we offer our "pedagogies of possibility" (Kinloch, 2010, p. 188). We hope our stories provide impetus for generating practices that students will remember as they grow up to "respect and protect their own and others' human dignity" (Gay, 2010, p. 61). This is our privilege and responsibility as culturally relevant teachers. As Janice said:

> We have this opportunity as teachers. What are we going to do? Just being able to pinpoint injustices is the first thing. Do we recognize it? Do we shy away from it? Then we must ask: Who are our students? Who are *we*? How did we develop our views of the world? Change begins with understanding ourselves and our students. Then we have to ask what we need to do differently to create more equitable places in our classrooms and the world. You have this job to do that's all that. What are you going to do?

References

Adichie, C. (2009). Danger of the single story. *TED*. Retrieved from www.ted.com/talks/chimamanda_adichie_the_danger_of_a_single_story/transcript

Alexander, M. (2012). *The new Jim Crow: Mass incarceration in the age of colorblindness.* New York, NY: The New Press.

Alie, J. A. D. (1990). *A new history of Sierra Leone.* New York, NY: Macmillan.

Arie, I. (2016). Just for today. On *Testimony, volume 1: Life and relationship* [CD]. Santa Monica, CA: Universal.

Asante, M. K. (1992). Afrocentric curriculum. *Educational Leadership, 49*(4), 28–31.

Asante, M. K. (2014). *Facing south to Africa: Toward an Afrocentric critical orientation.* New York, NY: Lexington Books.

Asante, M. K. (2017). *Revolutionary pedagogy: Primer for teachers of Black children.* New York, NY: Universal Write Publications.

Attie, B., Goldwater, J., & Gordon, S. S. (2016). *BaddDDD Sonia Sanchez* [TV movie]. Bala Cynwyd, PA: Attie & Goldwater Productions.

Au, W., Brown, A. L., & Calderón, D. (2016). *Reclaiming the multicultural roots of U.S. curriculum: Communities of color and official knowledge in education.* New York, NY: Teachers College Press.

Baker-Bell, A., Butler, T., & Johnson, L. (2017). The pain and the wounds: A call for critical race English Education in the wake of racial violence. *English Education, 49*(2), 116–119.

Baker-Bell, A., Stanbrough, R. J., & Everett, S. (2017, January). The stories they tell: Mainstream media, pedagogies of healing, and critical media literacy. *English Education,* 130–152.

Baldridge, B. (2017). "It's like this myth of the Supernegro": Resisting narratives of damage and struggle in the neoliberal educational policy context. *Race, Ethnicity, and Education, 20*(6), 781–795.

Baldwin, J. (1962). *Letter to my nephew.* Retrieved from progressive.org/magazine/letter-nephew/

Banks, J., & Banks, C. A. (2010). *Multicultural education: Issues and perspectives* (7th ed.). New York, NY: Wiley.

Basterra, M., Trumbull, E., & Solano-Flores, G. (2011). *Cultural validity in assessment: Addressing linguistic and cultural diversity.* New York, NY: Routledge.

Battiste, M. (2013). *Decolonizing education: Nourishing the learning spirit.* Saskatoon, Canada: Purich.

Bevins, D. K. (2010). What is internalized racism? In M. Potapchuk, S. Leiderman, & D. Bivens (Eds.), *Flipping the script: White privilege and community building* (pp. 43–51). Silver Spring, MD: Center for Assessment and Policy Development, MP Associates.

Billante, J., & Hadad, C. (2010). White and black children biased toward lighter skin. *CNN.* Retrieved from cnn.com/2010/US/05/13/doll.study/index/html

Bishop, R. S. (1990). Mirrors, windows, and sliding glass doors. *Perspectives: Choosing and Using Books for Your Classroom, 6*(3).

Blanchett, W. J. (2009). From *Brown* to the resegregation of African Americans in special education—It is time to "go for broke." *Urban Education, 44,* 370–388.

Boutte, G. (2016). *Educating African American students: And how are the children?* New York, NY: Routledge.

Boutte, G., & Hill, E. H. (2006). African American communities: Implications for culturally relevant teaching. *The New Educator, 2,* 311–329.

Boutte, G., Johnson, G., Wynter-Hoyte, K., & Uyoata, U. E. (2017). Using African diaspora literacy to heal and restore the souls of young Black children. *International Critical Childhood Policy Studies, 6*(1), 66–79.

Brown, A. (2018). Memory and racism. *Diverse Issues in Higher Education.* Retrieved from diverseeducation.com/article/107704/

Brown, K., & Brown, A. (2012, Winter–Spring). Useful and dangerous discourse: Deconstructing racialized knowledge about African-American students. *Educational Foundations,* 11–26.

Burton, O., & Cross, W. (2014). *Penn Center: A history preserved.* Athens, GA: University of Georgia Press.

Butler, T. (2017). #Say[ing] her name as critical demand: English education in the age of erasure. *English Education, 49*(2), 153–178.

Campbell, E. (2008). *Gullah cultural legacies: A synopsis of Gullah traditions, customary beliefs, art forms, and speech on Hilton Head Island and vicinal sea islands in South Carolina and Georgia.* Hilton Head: SC: Gullah Heritage Consulting Services.

Carney, J. A. (2001). *Black rice: The African origins of rice contributions in the Americas.* Cambridge, MA: Harvard University Press.

Carrier, T. (1990). *Family across the sea* [DVD]. Columbia, SC: SCETV.

Case, D., & Hunter, C. (2012). Counterspaces: A unit of analysis for understanding the role of settings in marginalized individuals' adaptive responses to oppression. *Am J Community Psychology, 50,* 257–270.

Castagno, A. E. (2014). *Educated in whiteness: Good intentions and diversity in schools.* Minneapolis, MN: University of Minnesota Press.

Caughy, M. O., O'Campo, P. J., & Mutaner, C. (2004). Experiences of racism among African American parents and the mental health of their preschool-aged children. *American Journal of Public Health, 94*(12), 2118–2124.

Clark, K., & Clark, M. (1947). Racial identification and preference among negro children. In E. L. Hartley (Ed.), *Readings in social psychology* (pp. 169–178). New York, NY: Holt, Rinehart, and Winston.

Coates, T. (2015). *Between the world and me.* New York, NY: Spiegel & Grau.

Coates, T. (2017). *We were eight years in power: An American tragedy*. New York, NY: One World.

Codrington, J., & Fairchild, H. H. (2013*). Special education and the mis-education of African American children: A call to action*. Washington, DC: The Association of Black Psychologists.

ColaDaily. (2016). Teachers tour school community to better understand students' lives outside the classroom. *ColaDaily*. Retrieved from www.coladaily.com/2016/08/15/ teachers-tour-school-community-to-better-understand-students-lives-outside-the-classroom/

Collins, P. H. (2000). *Black feminist thought*. New York, NY: Routledge.

Collopy, T. (2016). Agents of change: Educators partner to put students at the heart of the curriculum. *Council Chronicle, 26*(2), 6–9.

Cooper, A. J. (1892). *A voice from the south*. Xenia, OH: Aldine Printing House.

Cooperative Children's Book Center. (2017). Publishing statistics on children's books by and about people of color and first/native nations people. *Cooperative Children's Book Center*. Retrieved from ccbc.education.wisc.edu/books/pcstats.asp

Cowhey, M. (2006). *Black ants and Buddhists: Thinking critically and teaching differently in the primary grades*. Portland, ME: Stenhouse.

Davis, K. (2006). A girl like me. *YouTube.* Retrieved from www.youtube.com/ watch?v=EivX77ORIIs

Dee, T., & Penner, E. (2016). *The casual effects of cultural relevance: Evidence from an ethnic studies curriculum*. Palo Alto, CA: Center for Education Policy Analysis.

Delpit, L. (2012). *"Multiplication is for white people": Raising expectations for other people's children*. New York, NY: The New Press.

Derman-Sparks, L., & Edwards, J. O. (2010). Anti-bias education for young children and ourselves. Portland, ME: Stenhouse.

Derman-Sparks, L., & Ramsey, P. G. (2006). *What if all the kids are white?: Anti-bias multicultural education with young children and families*. New York, NY: Teachers College Press.

Dezol, C. (2010). *Black history is our history* [Streaming audio]. iTunes and Apple Music. Retrieved from itunes.apple.com/us/album/black-history-is-our-history-single/ 1328687352

Dillard, C. (2012). *Learning to (re)member the things we've learned to forget: Endarkened feminisms, spirituality, and the sacred nature of research and teaching*. New York, NY: Peter Lang.

Dillon, L., & Dillon, D. (2006). *Jazz on Saturday night*. New York, NY: The Blue Sky Press.

Diop, C. A. (1989). *The African origin of civilization: Myth or reality*. Chicago, IL: Chicago Review Press.

Dominguez, M. (2017). "Se hace puentes al andar": Decolonial teacher education as a needed bridge to culturally sustaining and revitalizing pedagogies. In D. Paris & S. Alim (Eds.), *Culturally sustaining pedagogies: Teaching and learning for justice in a changing world* (pp. 225–246). New York, NY: Teachers College Press.

Du Bois, W.E.B. (1903). *The souls of Black folk*. Chicago, IL: A.C. McClurg & Co.

Du Bois, W.E.B. (1920). *Darkwater: Voices from within the veil.* New York, NY: Harcourt Brace.

Dudley-Marling, C., & Lucas, K. (2009). Pathologizing the language and culture of poor children. *Language Arts, 86*(5), 362–370.

Dunbar-Ortiz, R. (2014). *An indigenous people's history of the United States.* Boston, MA: Beacon Press.

Duncan-Andrade, J. M., & Morrell, E. (2008). *The art of critical pedagogy: Possibilities for moving from theory to practice in urban schools.* New York, NY: Teachers College Press.

Edelsky, C. (2006). *With liberty and justice for all: Rethinking the social in language and education.* New York, NY: Routledge.

Edwards, B., & Rodgers, N. (1979). *We are family.* New York, NY: Cotillion.

Emdin, C. (2016). *For White folks who teach in the hood . . . and the rest of y'all too: Reality pedagogy and urban education.* Boston, MA: Beacon Press.

Ford, D. (2010). *Reversing underachievement among gifted Black students.* Waco, TX: Prufrock Press.

Ford, D. (2013). *Recruiting and retaining culturally different students in gifted education.* Waco, TX: Prufock Press, Inc.

Ford, J. E. (2015). We need to start telling the truth about White supremacy. *EducationPost.* Retrieved from educationpost.org/we-need-to-start-telling-the-truth-about-white-supremacy-in-our-schools/

Foster, M. (1997). *Black teachers on teaching.* New York, NY: The New Press.

Freire, P. (1970). *Pedagogy of the oppressed.* New York, NY: Continuum.

Gangi, J. (2008). The unbearable whiteness of literacy instruction: Realizing the implications of the proficient reader research. *Multicultural Review* (Spring, 2008), 30–35.

Gay, G. (2010). *Culturally responsive teaching: Theory, research, and practice.* New York, NY: Teachers College Press.

Gershenson, S., Holt, S. B., & Papageorge, N. W. (2016). Who believes me? The effect of student-teacher demographic match on teacher expectations. *Economics of Education Review, 52,* 209–224.

Gigliotti, D. (Producer), & Melfi, T. (Director) (2016). *Hidden figures* [Motion picture]. Fox 2000 Pictures, Chernin Entertainment.

Gilliam, W., Maupin, A., Reyes, C., Accavitti, M., & Shic, F. (2016*). Do implicit biases regarding sex and race relate to behavior expectation and recommendations of preschool expulsions and suspensions?* New Haven, CT: Yale University Child Study Center.

Gonzalez, N., Moll, L., & Amanti, C. (2005). *Funds of knowledge: Theorizing practice in households, communities, and classrooms.* Mahwah, NJ: Lawrence Erlbaum.

Gorski, P. (2008). Peddling poverty for profit: Elements of oppression in Ruby Payne's framework. *Equity and Excellence in Education, 41*(1), 130–148.

Greenfield, E. (1986). *Honey, I love and other love poems.* New York, NY: Harper Collins.

Gregory, E., Long, S., & Volk, D. (Eds.) (2004). *Many pathways to literacy: Young children learning with siblings, peers, grandparents, and communities.* London, England: RoutledgeFalmer.

Griffin, J. H. (1961). *Black like me.* New York, NY: Houghton-Mifflin.

Guisepi, (2001). Africa, the spread of civilization in Africa. *History-World.* Retrieved from history-world.org/africa1.htm

Guo, W., & Vulchi, P. (2016). *The classroom index.* Princeton, NJ: CHOOSE.

Haddix, M. (2016). *Cultivating racial and linguistic diversity in literacy teacher education: Teachers like me.* New York, NY/Urbana, IL: Routledge/NCTE.

Hamer, F. L. (1971, July 10). *Nobody's free until everybody's free.* Speech delivered at the Founding of the National Women's Political Caucus, Washington, DC.

Hapanyengwi-Chemhuru, O., & Makuvaza, N. (2014). Hunhu: In search of an Indigenous philosophy for the Zimbabwean education system. *Journal of Indigenous Social Development, 3*(1), 1–15.

Hart, B., & Risley, T. R. (2003). The early catastrophe: The 30 million word gap by age 3. *American Educator, 27*(1), 4–9.

Heard, G. (1998). *Awakening the heart: Exploring poetry in elementary and middle school.* Portsmouth, NH: Heinemann.

Hill, M. L. (2009). *Beats, rhymes, and classroom life: Hip-hop pedagogy and the politics of identity.* New York, NY: Teachers College Press.

Hill, M. L. (2016a). 3 elements underpinning education reform. *New Black Man (in Exile).* Retrieved from www.newblackmaninexile.net/2016/03/marc-lamont-hill-discusses-3-elements.html

Hill, M. L. (2016b). *Nobody: Casualties of America's war on the vulnerable, from Ferguson to Flint and beyond.* New York, NY: Atria.

Hilliard, A. G. (1998). *The reawakening of the African mind.* Gainesville, FL: Makare Publishing Co.

Hirschfeld, L. A. (2008). Children's developing conceptions of race. In S. M. Quintana & C. McKown (Eds.), *Handbook of race, racism, and the developing child* (pp. 37–54). Hoboken, NJ: John Wiley & Sons.

Hoffman, M. (1995). *Boundless Grace.* New York, NY: Puffin.

hooks, b. (1994). *Teaching to transgress: Education as the practice of freedom.* New York, NY: Routledge.

Howard, T. (2010). *Why race and culture matter in schools: Closing the achievement gap in America's schools.* New York, NY: Teachers College Press.

Howard, T. (2014). *Black male(d): Peril and promise in the education of African American males.* New York, NY: Teachers College Press.

Hughes-Hassell, S., Barkley, H. A., & Koehler, E. (2009). Promoting equity in children's literacy instruction: Using a critical race theory framework to examine transitional books. *School Media Research, 12.* Retrieved from www.ala.org/aasl/slr

Hunter, M. (2007). The persistent problem of colorism: Skin tone, status, and inequality. *Sociology Compass, 1*(1), 237–254.

Husband, T. (2016). *But I don't see color: The perils, practices, and possibilities of antiracist education.* Rotterdam, The Netherlands: Sense Publishers.

Jackson, T. O., & Howard, T. C. (2014). The continuing legacy of Freedom Schools as sites of possibility for equity and social justice for Black students. *Western Journal of Black Studies, 38*(3), 155–162.

Jenkins, T. (2013). De(re)constructing ideas of genius: Hip-hop, knowledge, and intelligence. *International Journal of Critical Pedagogy, 4*(3), 11–23.

Jennings, M. E., & Lynn, M, (2005). The house that race built: Critical pedagogy, African American education, and the re-conceptualization of a critical race pedagogy. *Educational Foundations, 19*(3–4), 15–32.

Jensen, R. (2005). *The heart of whiteness: Confronting race, racism, and white privilege.* San Francisco, CA: City Lights Publishers.

Johnson, D. (2007). *Hair dance.* New York, NY: Holt.

Johnson, L., & Bryan, N. (2016). Using our voices, losing our bodies: Michael Brown, Trayvon Martin, and the spirit murders of Black male professors in the academy. *Race Ethnicity and Education.* doi: 10.1080/13613324.2016.1248831

Kebede, A. (2017). *Roots of Black music: The vocal, instrumental, and dance heritage of Africa and Black America.* Trenton, NJ: Africa World Press.

Kelly, L. L. (2013). Hip-hop literature: The politics, poetics, and power of hip-hop in the English classroom. *English Journal, 102*(5), 51–56.

Kempner, A. (2015). *Rosenwald: A remarkable story of a Jewish partnership with African American communities.* Washington, DC: Ciesla Foundation.

Kendi, I. X. (2016). *Stamped from the beginning: The definitive history of racist ideas in America.* New York, NY: Nation Books.

Khan-Cullors, P., Garza, A., & Tometi, O. (2016). *What we believe.* Available at https://blacklivesmatter.com/about/what-we-believe/

Kinard, T., Gainer, J., & Heurta, M.E.S. (2018*). Power play: Explorando y empujando fronteras en una escuela tejas through a multilingual play-based early learning curriculum.* New York, NY: Peter Lang.

King, J. (1991). Dysconscious racism: Ideology, identity, and the miseducation of teachers. *The Journal of Negro Education, 60*(2), 133–146.

King, J., & Akua C. (2012). Dysconscious racism and teacher education. In J. Banks (Ed.), *Encyclopedia of diversity in education,* (pp. 724–727). Thousand Oaks, CA: Sage.

King, J., & Swartz, E. (2014). *"Re-membering" history in student and teacher learning: An Afrocentric culturally informed praxis.* New York, NY: Routledge.

King, J., & Swartz, E. (2016). *The Afrocentric praxis of teaching for freedom: Connecting culture to learning.* New York, NY: Routledge.

King, M. L. (1959). *Remaining awake through a great revolution.* Morehouse College Commencement Address.

Kinloch, V. (2010). *Harlem on our minds: Place, race, and the literacies of urban youth.* New York, NY: Teachers College Press.

Kinloch, V., & Dixon, K. (2017). Equity and justice for all: The politics of cultivating anti-racist practices in urban education. *English Teaching: Practice and Critique, 16*(3), 331–346.

Kirkland, D. (2016a). *A search past silence: The literacy of young black men.* New York, NY: Teachers College Press.

Kirkland, D. (2016b). *Centering students: How educators can fix schools and classrooms, a cultural relevance perspective.* Brown Bag Discussion: Metropolitan Center for Research on Equity and Transformation in Schools, New York University.

Kleinfeld, J. (1975). Effective teachers of Eskimo and Indian students. *School Review, 83,* 301–344.

Knoester, M., & Au, W. (2014). Standardized testing and school segregation: Like tinder for fire? *Race, Ethnicity, and Education, 20*(1), 1–14.

Kohli, R. & Solórzano, D. (2012). Teachers please learn our names: Racial microaggressions and the K–12 classroom. *Race, Ethnicity, and Education, 15,* 1–22.

Ladson-Billings, G. (1994). *The dreamkeepers: Successful teachers of African American children.* San Francisco, CA: Jossey-Bass.

Ladson-Billings, G. (1995a). Toward a theory of culturally relevant pedagogy. *American Educational Research Journal, 32*(3), 465–491.

Ladson-Billings, G. (1995b). But that's just good teaching!: The case for culturally relevant pedagogy. *Theory into Practice, 43*(3), 159–165.

Ladson-Billings, G. (2003). "I ain't writin 'nuttin'": Permissions to fail and demands to succeed in urban classrooms. In L. Delpit & J. K. Dowdy (Eds.), *The skin that we speak: Thoughts on language and culture in the classroom,* (pp. 107–220). New York, NY: The New Press.

Ladson-Billings, G. (2006). From the achievement gap to the education debt: Understanding achievement in U.S. schools. *Educational Researcher, 35*(7), 3–12.

Ladson-Billings, G. (2014). Culturally relevant pedagogy 2.0: a.k.a. the remix. *Harvard Educational Review, 84*(1), 74–84.

Ladson-Billings, G. (2017). The (r)evolution will not be standardized: Teacher education, hip hop pedagogy, and culturally relevant pedagogy 2.0. In D. Paris & S. Alim (Eds.), *Culturally sustaining pedagogies: Teaching and learning for justice in a changing world* (pp. 141–156). New York, NY: Teachers College Press.

Littlefield, D. (1991). *Rice and slaves: Ethnicity and the slave trade in colonial South Carolina.* Champaign, IL: University of Illinois Press.

Long, S. (2004). Passionless text and phonics first: Through a child's eyes. *Language Arts, 81*(5), 61–70.

Long, S., Abramson, A., Boone, A., Borchelt, C., Kalish, R., Miller, E., Parks, J., & Tisdale, C. (2006). *Tensions and triumphs in the early years of teaching: Real world findings and advice for supporting new teachers.* Urbana, IL: National Council of Teachers of English.

Long, S., Anderson, C., Clark, M., & McCraw, B. (2008). Going beyond our own worlds: A first step in envisioning equitable practice. In C. Genishi & A. L. Goodwin (Eds.), *Diversities in early childhood education: Rethinking and doing,* (pp. 253–272). New York, NY: Routledge.

Long, S., with Hutchinson, W., & Neiderhiser, J. (2011). *Supporting students in the time of Common Core Standards, 4K Through Grade 2.* Urbana, IL: National Council of Teachers of English.

Long, S., Souto-Manning, M., & Vasquez, V.M. (Eds.) (2016). *Courageous leadership in early childhood education: Taking a stand for social justice.* New York, NY: Teachers College Press.

Long, S., Volk, D., Baines, J., & Tisdale, C. (2013). "We've been doing it your way long enough": Syncretism as a critical process. *Journal of Early Childhood Literacy, 13*(3).

López-Robertson, J., Long, S., & Turner-Nash, K. (2010). First steps in constructing counter narratives of young children and their families. *Language Arts, 88*(2), 94–103.

Louw, D. J. (1998). Ubuntu: An African Assessment of the religious other. *The Padeia Project.* Retrieved from www.bu.edu/wcp/Papers/Afri/AfriLouw.htm

Love, B. (2015). What is hip-hop-based education doing in *nice* fields such as early childhood and elementary education? *Urban Education, 50*(1), 106–131.

Love, B. (2016). Anti-Black state violence, classroom edition: The spirit murdering of Black children. *Journal of Curriculum and Pedagogy, 13*(1), 1–3.

Luján, A. (2016). Social justice and the principled principal: All children are gifted. In S. Long, M. Souto-Manning, & V. M. Vasquez (Eds.), *Courageous leadership in early childhood education: Taking a stand for social justice* (pp. 113–124). New York, NY: Teachers College Press.

Lyiscott, J. (2017a, November). *The politics of ratchetness: Existing while being Black within and beyond the classroom.* Paper presented at the Cultivating New Voices Among Scholars of Color Institute, St. Louis, MO.

Lyiscott, J. (2017b). *Pedagogy on fire! Is your classroom defeated, defined, or developed in this era?* Portsmouth, NH: Heinemann. Retrieved from medium.com/@heinemann/pedagogy-on-fire-9991c63ae11c

Lyiscott, J. (2017c). Racial identity and liberation literacies in the classroom. *English Journal, 106*(4), 47–53.

Lytra, V., Volk, D., & Gregory, E. (2016). *Navigating languages, literacies, and identities: Religion in young lives.* London, England: Routledge.

Mahiri, J. (1998). *Shooting for excellence: African American and youth culture in new century schools.* Urbana, IL: National Council of Teachers of English.

Matias, C., & Liou, D. D. (2015). Tending to the heart of communities of color: Towards critical race teacher activism. *Urban Education, 50*(5), 601–625.

Mazama, A., & Lundy, G. (2012). African American homeschooling as racial protectionism. *Journal of Black Studies, 43*(7), 723–748.

McCarrier, A., Pinnell, G., & Fountas, I. (1999). *Interactive writing.* Portsmouth, NH: Heinemann.

McCarty, T., & Lee, T. (2014). Critical culturally sustaining/revitalizing pedagogy and indigenous education sovereignty. *Harvard Educational Review, 84*(1), 101–124.

McCormack, S. (2018, February 1). Why every student needs "permission" to be brilliant and how we can give it to them. *Courier-Journal.* Retrieved from www.courier-journal.com/story/opinion/2018/02/01/black-history-jefferson-county-public-schools-teacher/1016664001/

McCraw, B. (2014). *There is an app for that: Uses of print and digital materials in the lives of three preschoolers* (Unpublished doctoral dissertation). University of South Carolina, Columbia, SC.

McMillon, G. T., & Edwards, P. A. (2000). Why does Joshua "hate" school . . . but love Sunday School? *Language Arts, 78*(2), 111–120.

Miller, E. (2015). Race as the Benu: A reborn consciousness for teachers of our youngest children. *Journal of Curriculum Theorizing, 30*(30), 28–44.

Mills, H. (2005). It's all about looking closely and listening carefully. *School Talk, 11*(1), 1–3.

Milner, R. (2015). *Rac(e)ing to class: Confronting poverty and race in schools and classrooms.* Cambridge, MA: Harvard Education Press.

Monroe, C. (2017). *Race and colorism in education.* New York, NY: Routledge.

Morrell, E. (2015). *Powerful English at NCTE yesterday, today, and tomorrow: Toward the next movement.* Urbana, IL: National Council of Teachers of English.

Morris, M. W. (2016). *Pushout: The criminalization of Black girls in schools.* New York, NY: The New Press.

Muhammad, G., & Haddix, M. (2016). Centering Black girls' literacies: A review of literature on multiple ways of knowing of Black girls. *English Education, 48*(4), 299–336.

Myers, M. (2013, May). Finding common concerns for the children we share: Rural and Black families may support their child's education in ways that differ from middle class. *Phi Delta Kappan, 94*(8), 39–44.

Nash, K., Panther L., & Arce-Boardman, A. (2017). *La historia de mi nombre*: A culturally sustaining early literacy practice. *The Reading Teacher.* Retrieved from doi. org/10.1002/trtr.1665

Nieto, S. (2010). *The light in their eyes: Creating multicultural learning communities* (10th anniversary ed.). New York, NY: Teachers College Press.

Nieto, S. (2017). On reconciling divergent ideas: A life-long quest. *Education Review, 24*.

Noguera, P. (2014). *Schooling for resilience: Improving the life trajectory of Black and Latino boys.* Cambridge, MA: Harvard University Press.

Obama, B. (2015). *Remarks by the President in eulogy for the Honorable Reverend Clementa Pinckney.* Retreived from obamawhitehouse.archives.gov/the-press-office/2015/06/26/ remarks-president-eulogy-honorable-reverend-clementa-pinckney

Painter, N. I. (2011). *The history of white people.* New York, NY: W. W. Norton.

Paris, D. (2012). Culturally sustaining pedagogy: A needed change in stance, terminology, and practice. *Educational Researcher, 41*(3), 93–97.

Paris, D., & Alim, S. (2017). *Culturally sustaining pedagogies: Teaching and learning for justice in a changing world.* New York, NY: Teachers College Press.

Patel, L. (2016). *Decolonizing educational research: From ownership to answerability.* New York, NY: Routledge.

Payne, R. (2005). *A framework for understanding poverty.* Highlands, TX: Aha!Process.

Perkins, U. E. (2017). *Hey black child.* New York, NY: Little, Brown.

Perry, T., Steele, C., & Hilliard, A. (2004). *Young, gifted, and Black: Promoting high achievement among African American students.* Boston, MA: Beacon Press.

Pinkney, E. (2002). *Ella Fitzgerald: The tale of a vocal virtuosa.* New York, NY: Hyperion.

Ray, B. D. (2015). *Research facts on homeschooling.* Salem, OR: National Home Education Research Institute.

Ray, K. W. (2001). *The writing workshop: Working through the hard parts (and they're all hard parts).* Urbana, IL: National Council of Teachers of English.

Regan, P. (2010). *Unsettling the settle within: Indian residential schools, truth telling, and reconciliation in Canada.* Vancouver, Canada: University of British Columbia Press.

Roediger (2007). *The wages of whiteness: Race and the making of the working class.* Brooklyn, NY: Verso.

Rosner, J. (2011). The SAT: Quantifying the unfairness behind the bubbles. In J. Soares (Ed.). *SAT Wars: The case for test-optional college admissions,* (pp. 104–117). New York, NY: Teachers College Press.

Salazar, M. (2013). A humanizing pedagogy: Reinventing the principles and practice of education as a journey toward liberation. *Review of Research in Education, 37,* 121–148.

Sealey-Ruiz, Y. (2017). Understanding teacher as advocate. *YouTube.* Retrieved from www.youtube.com/watch?v=xL78f-1Ng3Q

Sealey-Ruiz, Y. & Haddix, M. (2016). Education *as if* Black lives mattered. Special edition of the American Educational Research Association (AERA) Division B Newsletter. Retrieved from www.academia.edu/22663442/Getting_Schooled_A_Curriculum_of_Lying_Choking_and_Dying_Special_Issue_of_the_Division_B_Newsletter_Black_Lives_Matter_full_issue_B._Wozolek_Ed._

Siddle Walker, V. (1996). *Their highest potential: An African American school community in the segregated south.* Chapel Hill, NC: University of North Carolina Press.

Siddle Walker, V., & Snarey, J. R. (2004). *Racing moral formation: African American perspectives on care and justice.* New York, NY: Teachers College Press.

Singer, S. (2016). Standardized tests have always been about keeping people in their place. *Gadfly on the wall.* Retrieved from gadflyonthewallblog.wordpress.com/2016/04/05/standardized-tests-have-always-been-about-keeping-people-in-their-place/

Skerrett, M. (2014). Dismantling colonial myths: Centralising Māori language in education. In J. Ritchie & Skerrett, M. (Eds.). *Early childhood education in Aotearoa New Zealand: History, pedagogy, and liberation* (pp. 10–34). New York, NY: Palgrave Macmillan.

Smith, C. (2016). The danger of silence. *YouTube.* Retrieved from www.youtube.com/watch?v=NiKtZgImdlY

Smith, L. T. (1999). *Decolonizing methodologies: Research and Indigenous peoples* (2nd ed.). London, England: Zed.

Smith-Buster, E. E. (2015). Social justice literature and writing: The case for widening our mentor texts. *Language Arts, 94*(2), 108–111.

Smitherman, G. (1977). *Talkin and testifyin: The language of Black America.* Detroit, MI: Wayne State University Press.

Soulja Boy. (2010). Pretty boy swag. On *the DeAndre way* [CD]. Santa Monica, CA: Universal.

Southern Poverty Law Center. (2016). Hatewatch. *Southern Poverty Law Center.* Retrieved from www.splcenter.org/hatewatch

Souto-Manning, M. (2007). Honoring children's names and, therefore, their identities. *School Talk, 12*(3), 1–2.

Souto-Manning, M., Llerena, C., Martell, J., Salas, A., & Arce-Boardman, A. (2018). *No more culturally irrelevant teaching.* Portsmouth, NH: Heinemann.

Souto-Manning, M., & Martell, J. (2016). *Reading, writing, and talk: Inclusive teaching strategies for diverse learners, K–2.* New York, NY: Teachers College Press.

Stone, A. (2006). *Brotha* [CD]. New York, NY: J Records.

Stovall, D. (2006). We can relate: Hip-hop culture, critical pedagogy, and the secondary classroom. *Urban Education, 41*(6), 585–602.

Sue, D. W. (2015). *Race talk and the conspiracy of silence: Understanding and facilitating difficult dialogues on race.* New York, NY: Wiley.

Tatum, A. (2009). *Reading for their Life: (Re)building the textual lineages of African American adolescent males.* Portsmouth, NH: Heinemann.

Tatum, B. D. (1997). *"Why are all the Black kids sitting together in the cafeteria?" and other conversations about race.* New York, NY: Perseus.

Thiong'o, N. (2005). *Decolonizing the mind: The politics of language in African literature.* Portsmouth, NH: Heinemann.

Trouillot, M. (1995). *Silencing the past: Power and the production of history.* Boston, MA: Beacon Press.

Tutu, D. (2011). *God is not a Christian and other provocations.* New York, NY: HarperOne.

United Nations Human Rights Council. (2016, 19–29 January). Statement to the media by the United Nations' working group of experts on people of African descent, on the conclusion of its official visit to the USA. Retrieved from www.ohchr.org/EN/NewsEvents/Pages/DisplayNews.aspx?NewsID=17000

U.S. Department of Education Office for Civil Rights. (2014). Retrieved from www2.ed.gov/policy/gen/guid/school-discipline/index.html

U.S. Department of Justice. (2016). Retrieved from ucr.fbi.gov/hate-crime/2016/topic-pages/incidentsandoffenses.

Van Wyk, B., & Higgs, P. (2012). The future of university research in Africa. In R. Barnett (Ed.), *The future university: Ideas and possibilities* (pp. 178–186). New York, NY: Routledge.

Vasquez, V. (2014). *Negotiating critical literacies with young children.* New York, NY: Routledge.

Watkins, W. H. (2001). *The White architects of Black education: Ideology and power in America, 1865–1954.* New York, NY: Teachers College Press.

Wayman, E. (2011). How Africa became the cradle of humankind. *Smithsonian Magazine.* Retrieved from www.smithsonianmag.com/science-nature/how-africa-became-the-cradle-of-humankind-108875040/

Waziyatawin, A. W., & Yellow Bird, M. (2005). *For Indigenous eyes only: A decolonization handbook.* Santa Fe, NM: School for Advanced Research Press.

Weldon, T. (2003). Copula variability in Gullah. *Language Variation and Change, 15*(1), 37–72.

Williams, T. M. (2011). *Black teachers caring for Black students: Intersecting identity, culturally responsive teaching, and life history.* (Doctoral dissertation). University of North Carolina, Greensboro.

Willis, K. (2017). "Hidden figures" director defends decision to add fictitious White savior scenes to movie. *Atlanta Black Star.* Retrieved from atlantablackstar.com/2017/02/01/hidden-figures-director-defends-decision-add-fictitious-white-savior-scenes-movie/

Winkler, E. N. (2009). Children are not colorblind: How young children learn race. *PACE, 3*(3), 1–8.

Woodson, C. G. (1933). *The mis-education of the Negro*. Trenton, NJ: Africa World Press.

Wyman, L., & Kashatok, G. (2008). Getting to know students' communities. In M. Pollock (Ed.), *Everyday anti-racism: Getting real about race in school* (pp. 299–304). New York, NY: The New Press.

Wyatt, J. E. The Nannie Helen Burroughs project: Rebuilding a culture of character. Retrieved from nburroughsinfo.org.

Yosso, T. J. (2005). Whose culture has capital? A critical race theory discussion of community cultural wealth. *Race, Ethnicity, and Education, 8*(1), 69–91.

Zinn, H. (2015). *A young people's history of the United States: Columbus to the war on terror*. London, England: Seven Stories Press/Triangle Square.

Index

About the Authors

Janice Baines has 10 years of experience in early childhood education teaching preschool, kindergarten, first, and second grades as well as working in and developing afterschool and summer programs, as a Reading Interventionist, a research assistant, and supervisor of student teachers. She received her bachelor's degree in Early Childhood Education from Benedict College in Columbia, SC and her master's degree in Curriculum and Instruction from the University of Wisconsin-Milwaukee. She is a past Trustee of the National Council of Teachers of English (NCTE) Research Foundation and a recipient of NCTE's Early Career Educator of Color Leadership Award. She is the coauthor of articles focusing on culturally relevant teaching and her teaching was featured in Mariana Souto-Manning's *Multicultural Teaching in the Early Childhood Classroom* and Susi Long's *Supporting Students in a Time of Core Standards*. She has been involved with many professional memberships and as a presenter at numerous national and local education conferences.

Carmen Tisdale has 15 years of teaching experience in kindergarten, first, second, and third grades and as a Reading Interventionist. She received her master's degree in Early Childhood Education from the University of South Carolina. She has been honored as Teacher of the Year in her school and named as one of the five finalists for district Teacher of the Year. Her professional involvement includes serving as the Elementary Representative-at-Large on the Executive Committee of the National Council of Teachers of English (NCTE) and on the Governing Board for NCTE's Professional Dyads and Culturally Relevant Teaching project. She is coauthor of several articles focusing on culturally relevant teaching and coresearched and coauthored the book *Tensions and Triumphs in the Early Years of Teaching*, focusing on barriers and support in the lives of new teachers. Her teaching has been featured in Sonia Nieto's *Finding Joy in Teaching Students of Diverse Backgrounds* and in Susi Long's *Supporting Students In a Time of Core Standards*.

Susi Long is a past elementary school teacher and currently a Professor in the Department of Instruction and Teacher Education at the University of South Carolina. Her research, teaching, and inservice professional development focuses on culturally relevant, humanizing, and decolonizing pedagogies in early childhood, elementary, and preservice teacher education. Her books, written with teachers and university colleagues, include *Tensions and Triumphs in the Early Years of Teaching, Supporting Students in a Time of Core Standards, Many Pathways to Literacy,* and *Courageous Leadership in Early Childhood Education.* Susi teaches courses in literacy methods, culturally relevant pedagogies, linguistic pluralism, family-school dynamics, and critical qualitative research methods. She is past Chair of the Board of Trustees of the National Council of Teachers of English (NCTE) Research Foundation and cofounded NCTE's Early Childhood Education Assembly (ECEA) and the ECEA's *Professional Dyads and Culturally Relevant Teaching* project; she has held other NCTE leadership roles. She is the 2013 recipient of the NCTE Early Childhood Education Assembly's *Early Literacy Educator of the Year* award and started her career as NCTE's 1997 *Promising Researcher.*